SINGLE MOM, BROKE
AND STILL SMILING

Catherine Oaks

TATE PUBLISHING
AND ENTERPRISES, LLC

Table of Content

Published by Tate Publishing & Enterprises, LLC
127 E. Trade Center Terrace | Mustang, Oklahoma 73064 USA
1.888.361.9473 | www.tatepublishing.com

Tate Publishing is committed to excellence in the publishing industry. The company reflects the philosophy established by the founders, based on Psalm 68:11,
"The Lord gave the word and great was the company of those who published it."

Published in the United States of America

ISBN: 978-1-62147-712-9
1. Self-Help, General
2. Body, Mind & Spirit, General
12.05.10

Acknowledgements

Over the years, some people have taught me, guided me and contributed to my spiritual growth and happiness. In some cases, they helped me survive the storms and made me believe that life was worth living.

To my parents, Nicole and Pierre, who have never stopped sharing deep love no matter what happened. You have always been here for me. Je ne serais rien sans vous. Merci!

To my daughter Adelle, who is my treasure and my forever love. You have taught me faith, strength and perseverance. You have given me the biggest joys and the courage to continue the journey. I love you baby.

To Gloria Massey, my wonderful friend and mentor who never forgets me even if I forget her. You are the voice that cheers me up. Thank you for being in my life.

To Tom Jacobs, who made me believe that men can be real and deep and wholesome. Your shadow is never too far away from mine. I treasure our friendship. Thank you for never giving up on me, even when I pushed you away.

To David Jackson, who stuck by me both emotionally and financially when I was going through the closing on my company. Dave, you were invaluable. I will repay you every dime.

To all my employers, who have given me a chance to learn about what truly matters in my life. Thank you for believing in me when you hired me.

To my grandparents who shared with me principles that have taken me through the most challenging times. I wish you were still here by my side. I will always miss you.

To God, who is my hero and the one I always turn to, day in and day out as I know you listen. I know you are here no matter what and I know that even though I sometimes don't like the turbulences of my journey, I trust that I am exactly where I need to be, learning all lessons of life for your glory.

And to you my readers, who are given me a chance to hopefully make a difference in your life. I sincerely hope I do as, in the end, it's really all that matters to me.

1.
REALITY SNAPSHOT

Are you ready to make a change and shift your bad habits to create new healthier ones? Are you done with suffering for not so good reasons but you can't seem to be able to get out of reliving the same pains over and over again?

Do you want to believe that things can actually change and that your path can become brighter, warmer, shinier and full of hope?

Are you part of the winners and the go-getters or will you ever remain a follower of gloom and doom in the herd of complainers and losers that have absolutely no guts to take real action and impact their and others' lives?

Do you want to rise to new levels of happiness that are right in front of your nose?

Are you ready to feel good and make it last longer than a few minutes? Are you a superstar woman waiting to be discovered?

If you recognize yourself in the above statements, this book is for you. Through fifteen observations I have made over the years, I want to show you that the light can come up again and that you can switch from feeling down and lost to feeling hopeful and positive. While I speak about those observations, I will give you some snapshots of my life and experiences that I am sure you will relate to. I have been traveling the world and have seen things I am certain you will enjoy reading about as I am hoping they will create some light and put a smile on your face.

We are sometimes so stuck by our own bad habits that we can't recognize them and keep doing the same things that have taken us where we are over and over again. Sounds familiar? Well if it does, welcome my friend. That was me not so long ago until a bright acquaintance of mine knocked me on the head and made me realize that my gears had been stuck on the same speed for too long. He also told me that, if I was serious about wanting to change my life and its outcome, it was time to wake up. First, I shook my head with disbelief. But then, with some reflection, I got it. He was right! A guy was right! Oh, Revelation!

I actually had been developing habits that were creating undesirable results. What was wrong with me? I thought I was pretty smart but I started doubting my E.Q* level. How could I expect different results if I kept doing the same old things? How could my life change if I did not change the little things I was doing every day? How could I expect different reactions from others if I kept presenting the same facial expressions? How could my well being improve if I did not alter negative reactions to my surroundings, to my environment and to the world?

Yes it is tough to admit sometimes but we are the result of what we do every minute of every day. We are the outcome of what we have been told, molded by our civilization that has been teaching us what we are supposed to be doing to make something out of our lives. Does that seem a little out of place nowadays? Excuse me but I think the universe has recently shown us that so many of those great principles have actually been dismantled, misused and misapplied and that we, the good people following the rules, have been robbed from everything that we had believed in.

"Save for your retirement – Put money in your savings account on a regular basis and you will be soon set for life – Purchase a home even if you really can't afford it – Buy insurance even though they will never pay you back when you need it – Trust the big corporations as they have been in business for so long,

*E.Q: Emotional Quotient

they'll never cheat you" – And so on and so forth!

Let's be realistic girls! Things have changed. Our safety is no longer. We can't seem to trust anyone or anything because we just went through a complete universal earthquake. Pieces of our earth have been thrown into the air and they are now slowly falling down trying to find their place. But like any earthquake, the pieces that have been moved never quite fall at the same place they came from. Thank God in this case as those pieces were misplaced from the beginning anyway.

So here is the good news. I believe that the pieces of our earth will be slowly positioning themselves and settling back into much better spots than they originally came from. I believe that what is happening right now is actually extremely positive, creating a much healthier stronger foundation that will honor the righteous ones, the honest ones, the open minded ones and the ones that know to appreciate what they have, be positive and move on to create better lives for themselves and others. I believe that this is now the time for women, strong, smart women that have developed the brains and the energy to be the leaders of today and the inspiration of tomorrow. I believe that the status of men will change drastically.

I believe that what we are seeing right now with men is the beginning of the slump to a very different destiny. The majority of them are no men, no real guys will real "cojones". Most of them now refuse to take any responsibility for their families. They follow whatever their wives say, they let their wives drive, their wives handle the financing, the cooking, the children, the family, etc. What is left for them to do? Just complain about how miserable and depressed they are. Poor babies! They need their mommies again.

Let's shift this now as my purpose is not to depress you. My purpose is the opposite. This is all great news girls. Hope is showing its face, more and more everyday! There is hope for you, for your community, your city and for our world. Together, we can and we will make this world a better, healthier, stronger place. As everything starts with you and your own very simple steps.

So, power women, are you ready? Here we go.

2.

A LITTLE BIT OF HISTORY
MINE THAT IS

I grew up in a very stiff French family with strong and rigid principles and all I wanted to do is disturb them, question them and rethink them. It was the old French countryside where all seemed settled, approved, admitted and confirmed. I was told to do things a certain way, to think certain thoughts and to just be like everybody else. But I was just the opposite. I wanted to question, to disturb and to discover different worlds. So what did I do to be able to do just that, I left. At 18, I flew away to discover the world and where did I land first? Here in the United States.

I wanted to become an actress. My father wanted me to become and engineer and I wanted to become an actress. This was probably the day I triggered his first liver problems! After such news, he couldn't swallow anymore. But I did just that. I studied for a full year in a theater school learning how to act. After that year, I really never acted anymore as I was sent back to the old, boring, static unsurprising world that I came from. I had succumbed to the family influence and was back into the "normal", the routine, the accepted.

Well I can tell you that I did everything I could to make it the best out of this then depressing situation. I graduated with an MBA with honors, I found a job as international sales director traveling the world to sell cast iron parts wandering in dirty factories under extreme temperatures wearing huge boots and a helmet trying to negotiate gigantic deals with the most chauvinistic males.

I got married (my first marriage that is) at the age of 25 and stayed in that state of "misbliss" (just created that word) for 6 months. I did not love him. I just did what my family told me to do one more time and screwed up one more time. I got pregnant with my amazing daughter from a still married guy (learned that detail too late!) who tried to commit suicide after I announced to him the "baby on board" news. First, he missed, which told me he was not really serious about achieving his goal and second, if I gave you all the details, you wouldn't believe me so I will pass.

I met my now ex-husband —the second one— while traveling to Taiwan. Yep, another state of "missbliss" that went through the trash. After a few years of living in Hong-Kong with him, I landed in the United States because of him, which was probably the only good thing a man actually did for me, and divorced him because of undesirable behavior he started to demonstrate towards me and my daughter.

As a single mom with a five-year-old daughter, I had to start a new journey. I found a great job, bought my first home and a nice car and had a pretty decent life for about six years. I made some great money but then created my own business (that's my entrepreneurial spirit) with a partner that became ill, struggling with life's challenges. After a few months, his sickness combined with the failing economy contributed to the company's closure, to the loss of all my savings, to the foreclosure of my house and my filing for personal bankruptcy, forcing me to start all over again.

Now, did I mention that my daughter's birth dad who is still alive at least physically as his mental is definitely damaged, never sent a dime for her? Although I attempted to include him in her life, he never found the courage and the guts to be a true dad and only succeeded in making her feel unworthy. Following all of that, I fell in love with yet another married guy (I don't learn anything, do I?) that made me believe "unbeknownst to himself" that he was "unhappy" in his marriage and on his way out when in fact he was not really there yet. Should I go on? I think you got the picture.

Why am I speaking about my past?

Because like you, I have been going through "stuff". I screwed up big time but I also learnt big time. Because all of us have gone through stuff. Because it happens to every one of us to have reasons to believe that no matter what we do, we are doomed to failure. Because after so many disappointments, we doubt ourselves and our ability to make anything good out of our lives. We create the belief and the certainty that things will never change, that no matter what we do, results will remain shitty and disappointing. And we give up.

This is why I decided to write this book. To have a straight, honest talk woman to woman because I know you can and I know you will.

**TO WAKE YOU UP.
TO SCREAM TO YOU TO NOT GIVE UP
FOR THE SAKE OF YOU, FOR
THE SAKE OF YOUR CHILDREN
AND FOR THE SAKE OF THE WORLD!**

There is hope. Always. But that hope will only show its face if you change the little things you do every day.

3.

15 REALITIES THAT CAN CHANGE YOUR LIFE

*"Never give up, for that is just the place
and time that the tide will turn."*
- Harriet Beecher Stowe

REALITY #1
BOUNCING BACK AFTER THE INITIAL
SHOCK OF DIVORCE

I know what it is to wake up in the morning after it dawns on you that you are actually going through a divorce or a separation from a long-time partner. I know how it feels to look at yourself and at your children and feel the fear like a sword stuck deep in your stomach, preventing you from eating, drinking or breathing fully. I know what it is to feel your head spinning, wondering if you are going to be able to walk straight or if the wind will push you down to the ground not knowing if you would ever find the strength to get back up. I know. I have been there.

I have been to places inside of me where I wished I was buried 200 miles down the earth where no one could ever find me and where I hoped all my sorrows and my pains would collapse. I have felt such grief that for a while, every morning I was falling down on my bathroom's carpet wanting to dig deep screaming my disarray and my anger to the earth, hoping some dirt monster would hit me on the head and put an end to my life. I was afraid of the past, of the present, and of the future. I feared my inability to react, to be strong for my child and to move on with my life. My life was grabbing me at the neck suffocating me. I had two choices: giving up or waking up.

One of the most difficult things, I found, as a woman and a mother, was to try to figure out what it is I had done wrong. Why didn't I succeed in my marriage? Why couldn't I find fulfillment and happiness? Was there a problem with me?

After my divorce, I was lucky to find a great job that allowed me to purchase a home and have a pretty descent life style. Still, I was facing the anger of my ex husband, of his family and of my own internal world. I was going through loneliness minute after minute, hour after hour, day after day. Being on my own was frightening. I had to constantly face myself. When I was going to bed at night, I was secretly hoping I would not wake up the next day as I did not want to face the pain of a new day. At one point, I just couldn't take it. I had to find an outlet. I had to force myself to get out of my ego and look around. I had to shift my thinking and stop focusing on my one little self. Otherwise, I knew, something bad was going to happen.

So I started reading books. They became my best friends, my companions. They were my escape, my opening to a new, better world. They helped me understand what I was going through. They increased my awareness of who I was. I had been lost in a breezy, cold horizon and I was not sure where I was supposed to go. The more I read, the more I realized how little I knew and the more I needed to learn.

Soon, I became fascinated about what my life could become, if I only shifted my ways. I quickly understood thanks to some amazing authors (Wayne Dyer, Dr. Robin Smith, Eckhart Tolle, Marianne Williamson, Esther & Jerry Hicks, Oriah, Don Miguel Ruiz, etc.) that it was my choice to take what I had learnt and build some new paths towards a better life. So if you are going through similar pains, here is what I'd like you to do.

1. **Go buy more self-help books** and/or tapes and start reading them religiously. One that has helped me tremendously is the Tony Robbins' tape "The Edge". His energy is contagious and he gave me hope and courage to move on and to make significant changes for myself.

2. **Join a service group** (Rotary club, Lion's club, Big Brothers, Big Sisters. etc). Attend all their meetings and get involved into helping out other people. You'd be surprised how helping others helps you. It takes the focus out of yourself and makes you realize that, after all, your own situation is not so bad. There is so much suffering out there.

3. **Walk at least 20 minutes every day** and focus on your breathing while you walk. Then, create some mantra in your breathing. I was repeating the following during my

daily walks: "Things will be great. My life is changing. I am a successful mother. I am a happy person. Thank you God".

4. **Stick around positive people** and stay away from anything negative that you don't have to be around. Example: Headline news. If you can avoid, do not watch the news until you are back to a strong and healthy mental state. News are 90 percent negative and bring very little information. In order to stay informed, use the Internet and select what you want to read and be exposed to. The more you protect your close environment from any negative energy, the quicker you will get back on your feet.

5. **If you have pets, spend more time with them**. Pets are the most balanced living creatures. They have a high sense of joy and will bring the deepest, most natural joy. What I have been doing regularly is take my two dogs and go spend time in nature with them. Between their energy and the peacefulness of nature, I come back completely reenergized and much calmer inside. If you don't have pets, go get one. Just make sure that before you do so, you will be able to dedicate the time and attention they deserve and need from you.

Can you do this? Does that sound reasonable to you? I promise you that if you follow these five principles and repeat them on a regular basis, you will feel 100 percent better. Be patient as it may take a few weeks to get used to those new habits but soon, they will become second nature. Give yourself a chance. A chance to truly be and live the life of the wonderful woman that I know you are.

Now, do you want a little bit of humor? I already told you that I had been married twice. What I didn't tell you is that my first marriage lasted just about six months. I had the most beautiful wedding with old cars, a gorgeous dress, 5-star restaurants and hotels and about 300 guests. My family was the wealthiest family of my city and my parents had invited the whole town. I had been dating my future husband for 5 years before I finally gave up to the family pressure to marry him. "*Catherine, you are 25 years old. Do you want to die alone? Get married. Come on. It is your time!*". Well, after a few times of those lines, I finally gave up. I married my "best friend". The only problem is that I realized that I was only marrying my "best friend" at the door step of my favorite Catholic church. Why do I always do those things? What is wrong with me?

I got out of the car, holding my father by the arm, going up the stairs one by one, and the door to my future suddenly opened up. Both physically and literally. I would have loved to spare the "literally" part but I did not. While my father was walking towards my future husband, I stopped him and told him I needed to talk to him. He said "*what is going on with you?*" (yeah, I know). I responded

"*Dad, I don't think I want to get married anymore!*" My dad chocked and squeaked "*What the hell are you talking about?*" (all this was in French by the way). I calmly repeated "*Dad, I don't think I want to get married to that man.*

*I don't think I love him. I don't feel it. I just want to run away.
Right now!"*. Now remember that I grew up in a family with
deep strong Catholic principles. Except for my mother
who was a total atheist, my father's family was going to
church every Sunday and following to the T the Catholic
preaching. So what happened next? My father told me to
"swallow whatever was stuck in my throat", to *"continue putting one foot after the other towards my future husband"* and to
"forget about whatever was happening again in my wild mind".
So I did. I did not find the guts to turn around and nicely
thank the big crowd that came to my wedding telling them
"sorry but I am not ready for this yet!" Even now, I wake up
at night wondering why I have never been able to say *"no"*
to my father.

Do you want to know what happened next? The wed-
ding took place as planned. I said *"yes"* and *"I do"*. I almost
threw up while doing so. I put on my poker face and for
the next few hours became the best actress on earth. After
all, I had received that actor training a few years prior in
a great acting school in Bethesda, Maryland so I knew exactly what to do. The ceremony went on, the dinner went
on and the whole night dancing went on. Yes, that's what
we do in France for weddings. We dance all night long
and end up the event with a French onion soup at 6 a.m.
the next day.

At the end of all of these great happenings, I went to
bed with my now husband, refused to have sex and woke
up the next morning telling him I had made the biggest

mistake of my life and that I wanted a divorce. He tried all he can to change the path of my thoughts telling me that I was just scared because this was new and that it will pass.

So, he took me on a honey moon to a nudist camp where my father had a little apartment. Yep, that was another one of my father's favorite past time and also the least expensive trip my cheap husband could think of. After seeing hundreds of sun-burnt male essentials fluttering around the camp's beaches, I now knew for sure that I didn't want to have to bear one more night with the man that called himself my new husband. I did not want him. I did not love him. I wanted a divorce! And six months later, I got it. I left him expressing regrets for what I had done to him but also pointing out that this was going to save him a lot of future heartaches. He had just escaped having a wife that would stop sleeping with him after 2 weeks of marriage. Well he then said that he would never love another woman again. That I was it. I did not completely understood his statement then but learnt a few months later that he was living with a man and crazy in love.

This experience proved to me that things happen for a reason. It demonstrated that there is a reason for the feelings we have and that if we ignore them, we are up to interesting times that will challenge us to become whole again. I faced mine head first and allowed myself and my husband to live the life we wanted to live, separately. I never saw him again. I just heard that he was happy and fulfilled. I knew I had done the right thing.

SO MY FRIEND, IF I HAVE ONE ADVICE TO GIVE YOU HERE, IT IS TO NEVER MARRY WITHOUT TRUE LOVE. LISTEN TO YOUR FEELINGS. DON'T GET MARRIED BECAUSE YOUR FAMILY TELLS YOU TO DO SO. MONEY WON'T RESOLVE WHAT YOU DON'T FEEL AND WORK WON'T ALLOW YOU TO FORGET IT. BE TRUE TO WHO YOU ARE AND LISTEN TO THE STILL VOICE WITHIN. IT IS ALWAYS WISE AND ALWAYS RIGHT. YOU JUST NEED TO LEARN TO RECOGNIZE IT AND TO ACKNOWLEDGE IT. TRUST YOURSELF!

"Bah Hum Bug"
-Charles Dickens

REALITY #2
AHHHH, THE HOLIDAYS!

One of the most difficult moments for me as a single mom has been facing the holidays alone. I have resented the holidays for years. I chose to ignore them whenever possible. Do you feel the same way? Are you afraid of those few times of the year where your whole past jumps right at your face, making sure that all those moments that you spent together as a family are clearly coming back to your mind and kicking every inch of your memory?

Of course, when you have small children, you can't ignore those holidays. You can't ignore the turkey and the stuffing at Thanksgiving, Santa during Christmas, the gifts of Hanukkah or the Easter bunny and the chocolate Eggs. So what do you do? You fake the best smile you possibly can fake and just do it. However, deep inside, the pain is unbearable. That sword that was deeply stuck in your guts but that had settled in a steady position somehow, starts moving again. You are suffering in silence, trying to show behind your dark glasses all the pain you feel at that very moment.

This experience becomes even more interesting when you have to fake all of it in front of friends who invite you to their party, making sure that you would not be alone that day. I have had a few friends over the years that were just wonderful to me. They invited me to all of their family celebrations and did all they can to make sure that I would not spend a holiday alone. Although I genuinely appreciated their effort, I think in many occasions, it made everything even harder as it reinforced the fact that I did not have a family anymore. Or at least, my notion of family had been changed.

And here is the key word: Change. Only recently have I realized that a family is what you make of it. A family is not necessarily a wife, a husband, the kids, the grand-parents, the uncles and the aunts. A family is who-ever is close to your heart. You can create your own family again as long as you are willing to accept the "Change" in your own mind and shift the perception that you have created all these years. Because it is only perception. A little bit like a dream. We create our own reality.

Do you know that according to some Buddhist teachings, none of it is real. It is all a creation of our mind and even our mind itself is unreal. That is why I believe that even the attachment to the known and to our own identity is completely futile. Buddhists believe that we don't take all of this into our next life. "What we are today comes from our thoughts of yesterday and our present thoughts build our life of tomorrow. Our life is the creation of our mind". This comes from the Buddhist book *The Dhammapada*.

I believe that to be true as I now consciously exercise this process every single day of my life. I know how challenging it is to recognize our old patterns, assimilate them and consciously decide to break them. But for me, this was the only thing that took me away from the pains I was experiencing each time the calendar reached the word holiday. Now, I can't tell you that I look forward to them, I fly over them with calm and determination and they don't impact my emotions whatsoever. I know that soon I will actually start enjoying them.

Are you willing to shift? Are you ready to make some changes to give your heart a chance to be in a healthier, less painful place during those special days of the year? If so, here is what you need to do:

1. **Scream your pain out.** I know it sounds crazy but crazy measures work for crazy feelings and we are dealing with those right now. If the pain is unbearable, wait until you are home alone, close all windows and all doors and scream out loud. Let it out. Cry it out. Do all you can to get all those negative energies out of your body.

2. **Recognize your disdain for the holidays** and self affirm I understand that I don't like the holidays for such and such reason (write down all the reasons why you don't like them).

3. **Now apply the Buddhist theory** that your feelings are the creation of your mind. They are not real. Imagine those feelings floating on clouds and slowly flying away with the wind to never come back. Visualize that. Let go of all the reasons why you do not like the holidays. Just let them go peacefully.

4. **Repeat these steps as many times as needed until your habits are changed for good.**

Yes it may feel strange at first. But it works. Remember that we are creatures of habits and that it takes courage and determination to change those habits. Change is painful. It is your choice however to create a shift that is positive.

This notion of change, shift and perception was first presented to me when I was traveling to the Eastern countries (Bahrein, Dubai, the United Emirates, Saudi Arabia, etc.). I went there several times in my late twenties. Traveling to those areas of the world taught me the difference in orientation of the mind between the West and the East. It made me curious and I started researching what it was all about. I found out the following:

The West (us), represented by science, starts with what is knowable, visible or verifiable. This implies that science is limited by the power of the telescope or the microscope. As more powerful ones are made, many scientific truths have to be changed. Think about it. The earth was once thought to be flat with the sun revolving around it. The atom was once thought to be indivisible and so on. On the other hand, the East (the other side of us), begins with that which is unknowable, invisible and beyond sensory verification. In other words, it starts with the infinite and works toward the finite. The order is unlimited. Science begins with the finite and leaves the infinite out of the equation.

If I translate this into English, it means that it is critical to open our minds enough to be able to accept differences and different approaches to everything that has been taught to us. We have been taught either by the West or by the East and our knowledge has been molded to be fitting a certain direction. Now, what if we decided that our knowledge was not the truth and that we consciously can make the choice to be open-minded enough to consider the other way of thinking? What results would that create in our lives? Pretty fascinating I think.

Think of it now. The goal of the world of visibility is very relative (satisfaction of desires) while that of the world of invisibility is absolute (awareness of oneness). This is why the West and the East have so very little in common. This is why it is so very hard for us Western tribes to accept the Eastern tribes points of view and affirmations. We lack that "global" perspective of life and the living. Could we ever grab the two and bring them together? What would that result be?

Have I lost you yet? But seriously, could you imagine making yourself small enough in relation to an electron as you are in relation to the earth? Could you then change your scale of observation? Probably so. The more challenging question is "would you be willing to take that risk?"

All of this theory is to emphasize the fact that nothing is constant or forever. Everything that we are, that we see and that we touch is in constant movement and changes by the millisecond. A constant evolution of the matter. We are matter so we evolve and we live better and longer if we do actually evolve. Although change is painful, it is therefore necessary to grow and reach better places. Every day, cells die and give place to new ones. To conclude this chapter with something for you to remember and apply more on a subconscious level (as yes we do actually have certain power over our subconscious), everything is a matter of perspective.

It is not the event that is really hurting you. It is the way you perceive and react to that event.

This is difficult to understand at first as your body is already conditioned to react in a certain way, the way you have been taught for years. However, your body and especially your mind, can be conditioned to receive waves of pain in a different fashion. Your brain can be worked out to receive waves of information that are more positive, creating energies that you did not know you had.

My dear friend, you do have the ability to become strong after being deeply hurt. It only depends on how you decide to uncondition your body and your mind to receive information and welcome events.

WE, HUMANS, HAVE UNLIMITED POTENTIAL. OFTEN, STATES OF SUFFERING AND QUESTIONNING HELP US REALIZE WHAT OUR POTENTIAL IS AND GIVE US THE STRENGTH AND THE PERSPECTIVE TO CREATE ACTION PLANS THAT TAKE US BEYOND THE COMFORT-ABLE, TOWARDS INCREDIBLE HEIGHTS AND DISCOVERIES. ALLOW YOUR VISIONS TO BE AS WIDE AS THE WORLD. BELIEVE IN YOUR ABILI-TIES AND THE WORLD WILL OPEN ITSELF TO YOU, WITH ALL ITS WONDERS AND MIRACLES.

"Praise and blame,
gain and loss,
pleasure and sorrow
come and go like the wind.
To be happy, rest like a great tree
In the midst of them all"
-The Buddha

REALITY #3
LOW SELF-ESTEEM & VULNERABILITY

Low self-esteem is another source of tension that will prevent you from fully reaching happiness and peace. Self-esteem is a very delicate concept. It can take years to develop and it can be damaged in the snap of your fingers.

One of the biggest hurdles I had to face after my divorce was my self-esteem. I questioned and doubted everything about myself. I was weak and vulnerable but I was not totally conscious about it. I was not conscious of it but the outside world could see it as clearly as the clear deep blue waters of the Pacific Ocean. Now, do you know what happens in nature when the weak are obvious? They are devoured by the strong. The strong healthy species recognize the weak ones and go after them because they are the easy targets. They know and sense the path of least resistance to feed themselves.

Just like animals, humans react in the same fashion. When you are weak, you broadcast the weak signals, you emit negative energy and you unknowingly become a pray to the hungry beasts.

Let me give you an example. I went through a few things in my life that put me in that total pray pattern. The divorce was one of them. Another one was the closure of my business, the loss of my job and the bankruptcy filing I was forced to go through. I clearly remember how lost I was that first week where I did not go to the office as the office did not exist anymore. That Monday, I had to go visit an old customer who needed some help with his website. So I got dressed as I would on a normal work day, put make up on to look as good as I possibly could and forced a smile on my face, when the only thing I really wanted to do was cry. I felt like a loser. I had worked so hard at building my business and I had given it all. All my energy, all my beliefs and all my savings. Now, I had lost it all. I felt like I had nothing. I was completely lost, in a daze. I never took any drugs but I felt dizzy all the time. My brain was not able to function. I couldn't remember anything. Focusing was impossible.

I was controlled by my fear. My faith was pushed down by the negative thoughts scattered in my mind. My soul was unreachable. I could not eat normally and I spent most of my nights shivering, sweating, scared, while wondering how I could possibly face another day, let alone the future. So, that Monday, I got up, got into my car and visited that customer. He knew that my business had just closed but chose to ignore it. He greeted me like he had always greeted me. We took care of business and I left after a few minutes. You know, during those times when you feel so alone and so down, you hope that people will see it and land you a hand. But most people don't. Most people are too focused on their own life to even notice that you are not doing so well. I was hoping to find helping hands. I was so in need of them but none of them were reaching towards me. So I left that customer's place with disappointment and sorrow. Then, back into my car, something, a feeling, told me to go have coffee at the Starbucks next to my house. I normally don't do that but I just didn't feel like going back home and face myself and my loneliness. A strong sense and a presence just pushed me there.

So I drove to that destination knowing that something was there for me. I had no idea what it was. I just knew. I arrive at that Starbucks, park my car and walk towards the entrance. I push the door and notice quite a few people filling up the space. A gorgeous African American male sitting alone at the handicap table is reading paperwork. He has tens of documents piled up on the table and is reading them taking notes. As I am walking by, he lifts his head up and looks at me. I look at him back and something like never before happened. Thunder Strike. Love at first sight is another denomination of this type of happening. I look into his eyes. He looks into mine. I can see his soul and right there, all I want is to dive deep into him and never leave him.

Of course, I couldn't do that, so I continued my path towards the counter where I would order my coffee and croissant. Once I got them in my hands, and instead of leaving right there as I would have done any other time, I decided to stay a little longer. Interestingly enough, the table right next to him just became vacant. So I grabbed a newspaper and sat down drinking my coffee and reading.

Was I really reading? I can't remember a line of what was written. Not even the headlines. I was completely taken by that man and hoped that somehow, we would make a connection. He was very friendly to everyone and people were naturally talking to him. A lady he knew came towards him and started talking. I listened with intense curiosity. What would I find out?

Well, it appeared that he was working for a national organization and he was just taking a break from the office, at Starbucks. Don't we all do that? He had a sultry voice. I could sense some artist in him. A well hidden artist as he carried this very professional look, completely focused on his daily assignment.

The lady left and I was still there, reading my newspaper, or faking to do so. After a few minutes of complete silence, I could feel his eyes peeking towards my direction. And then he said:

"And what are you doing?" I replied faking total surprise.

"Who? Me?"

"Yes, you. I don't see anybody else here right now!!!" he answered with a smile.

"Oh, I am not sure what I am doing right now. I am kind of in-between things. I am looking for my next adventure, for a purpose right now".

"Hmmm" he replied "And what were you doing before you in-between state?" he asked

"I had my own business. An ad. agency. I was providing branding and marketing services focusing on utilizing new technologies to communicate to the world"

"Wow" he commented. "I may need your services. I am working on creating my own training company and I have no clue where to start with branding, or even marketing"

"Really?" I reacted with great interest. "I probably could help you. That would give me a purpose. I need a real purpose right now."

"OK. So what is your name and what is your phone number? I will call you and we can get together to speak business".

I gave him both. I got up, grabbed my newspaper and said good-bye. While I was leaving, I noticed a ring on his left hand. He was married. OK, I said to myself. I will only speak business with that guy, even though I am crazy attracted to him. I won't go there. Just business.

Now, you must wonder why I'm telling you this now. Well, we are in the low self-esteem and vulnerability chapter, right? I had low self-esteem and I was as vulnerable as one can be when I met that man. Yes there is a lot more to it but that man sensed that I was vulnerable. He sensed that I was in pain. All his body hormones were pushing him to act towards me and do something. So he did. Whether it was with a good intent or not, I did not know then. Only he did. I knew though that I gave my contact information to a total stranger and set up a "business" date with him while I had absolutely no idea who he was. He could have been the biggest sex offender of that area. He could have had terrible intentions. I put myself at risk, because I was weak. Oh was he irresistible to me. I could not understand why I was suddenly so attracted to him. I forced myself to push any romantic idea away. He was married. I did not want a married man.

So here is my point. You need to recognize that you are weak. Below are my tricks to recognize weakness and what you need to do when that happens:

1. **Recognize that you are in that state of weakness.**
   How do I know that? you would ask. Let's see!

- You cry often
- You are always tired
- You can't sleep well at night
- You are not hungry at all or on the contrary you can't stop eating
- You have thoughts of suicide
- You have thoughts of getting drunk because it hurts so much and you are looking for an outlet
- Everything scares you
- You are very irritable with your children
- You can't stand your pets anymore
- You break things around you
- You can't focus
- You don't want to get out of bed in the morning
- You blame Sylvia Brown for not telling you that this was going to happen to you.
- Even Jeff Dunham and Achmed the Dead Terrorist can't make you laugh! (are you laughing yet?) Jeff, by the way, thank you. You turned my lonely evenings into great stomach pains because of too much laughing!

2. **Create a shield to protect yourself**

Now, that does not mean not talking to anybody any more. It means watch out for the vultures that are going to sense your vulnerability. Do not give out your personal information too quickly as you will be tempted to, I promise you. Why would you be tempted to?

Because it makes you feel important and feeling important is a feeling we need to feel when we are depressed with low self-esteem. So, in those states of weakness, be extra careful with everyone you don't know. Again, that does not mean turning into a total asocial individual and not talking to anyone. No, it means just being extra selective. Don't give phone numbers but take phone numbers if you want to. That keeps you in control. Because you don't want anyone to control you.

3. Find anything you can to CALM DOWN and focus within.

Now, I have tried numerous things and some that worked for me may not work for you. You have to find what works for you. We are all different from one another. Here is what I recommend you do:

- Find a river somewhere or go to the ocean if you live near by one. Sit down next to it and listen to the sound of water while closing your eyes. Focus on your breathing while doing so and empty your brain. Try not to think of anything. Focus on your breathing. Yes I know I am repeating myself but I insist on this one. It is critical. Stay in that state for at least 20 minutes.

- Join a meditation group and meditate as often as you can. The group will teach you meditation techniques that you can apply at home on your own. At home, create an area for your meditation. Place on the wall pictures of people you respect, people you admire and who inspire you. I created my area and placed on my wall (or shelves if you don't have a wall in that specific area) photos of Jesus, of James Robbins, of Meryl Strip ~ what an amazing woman~ and of other people that bring life into me. Once this is done, buy incense and burn it while you meditate. Play some meditation music and meditate at least once a day (20 minutes minimum). This exercise will help you get centered and calm down.

4. Build up your faith

Faith is what helped me keep my sanity. I believe in God. I believe in higher powers. I believe in something stronger than all that we are. I believe in the righteousness of the universe and that good things happen to good people. What you are going through is necessary for you. You have to believe that you are exactly where you are supposed to be. It is hard to admit it when you are going through so much pain. But pain is the essence of your growth and your happiness. The lower you will fall the higher you will rise. It is the rule of the global spectrum leading you as an atom that changes every second to finally find a place where all feels good, all feels right for a complete enlightenment. Those exercises will help you feel calmer inside. You will be amazed as to how much you will gain from them. You will acquire better knowledge of yourself, better understanding of what you are going through and better acceptance of your situation. Remember, your situation is temporary. It won't last forever. I know it feels like it but it won't. I heard this once and it has helped me *"When you are going through hell, don't stop"*.

Makes sense, doesn't it? So, if you are going through hell, the best thing to do is to do everything you can to grow personally and spiritually so that you can move to better places, and you will.

LEARN ABOUT YOUR ROOTS, YOUR ANCESTORS, THEIR VALUES, THEIR LIVES. FROM THAT, YOU WILL GROW STRONGER, MORE CENTERED, MORE DETERMINED AND BETTER FOCUSED. AND, YOU WILL STRENGTHEN YOUR SELF-CONFIDENCE. NO SUCCESS IS ENDLESS.

NO DEFEAT IS UNCHANGEABLE.

ADVENTURE IS AT YOUR FINGERTIPS, ALWAYS, AS LONG AS YOU BELIEVE. TAKE IT ON, FULLY AND UNCONDITIONALLY AND BECOME A FLYING STAR.

"Children make you want to start life over"
-Muhammad Ali

REALITY #4
THE CHALLENGE OF SINGLE-PARENTHOOD

Being a parent is hard. Nobody teaches us parenting techniques. I have never had a course on parenting in High School or in college, and I didn't have to have a degree in parenting to qualify for any jobs I've applied to. Have you? I didn't think so.

You may or may not have children yet but if you do, you know what I mean. We learn on our own. We do everything we can to be a good parent. We experience incredible joy and incredible pain. In the end, we hope that our children will turn out to be happy, balanced and successful adults.

Our children often find themselves in the middle of turmoil as the family is torn part, going through divorce or other dramatic event. They suffer and we develop extreme guilt feeling we have failed them. So we compensate by spoiling them and we let go of discipline principles that should be applied. It is hard as a single parent to be both a loving and disciplinary human being. We tend to either be one or the other. It is challenging to play the role of the mom and the one of the dad at the same time. Our children know it and take advantage of it.

My daughter was five years old when I left my husband. I left him because he had become physically violent towards her. It happened first when she was three years old and when that happened, I clearly stated to him that if this happened another time, I would leave him.

I met my husband when I was three month pregnant with my daughter. My daughter's father was out of the picture unable and unwilling to share our lives. Here is how all of this started after we came back from a trip to Las Vegas.

Fall of 1994

"I need to talk to you" I said "I have cooked a great dinner for you. Please come sit down and spend a little time with me".

He sat downs. He finally looked at me and asked: "What is the matter love?". He used to call me "love", which warmed my heart so much.

"I have something to tell you that is very important. I don't know how you will react but now is the time. You know I love you and always have. We are celebrating tonight something you will remember the rest of your life."

I paused for a few seconds having somehow a hard

time pulling out the words that were sticking to my throat. "Antoine, I am pregnant with your child. We are going to have a baby".

Silence suddenly invaded the whole room. Antoine did not say a word. This news had hit him like thunder hits the ground and he did not know what to do or say. I felt scared and lost of his lack of reaction.

"Are you OK?" I carefully asked. "Aren't you happy about this?"

"I don't know " he finally answered. "I did not expect this to happen so quickly. This scares me to death. Why? Why now? I am not sure I am ready for this. Excuse me but I need to leave for a while. I can't stay here right now. I will call you"

He got up and started packing his clothes. Ten minutes later, he was gone.

At that very moment, I wanted to die, disappear from this cruel world. One more time, I had been struck by life. Antoine was gone and I knew that he would not be here for my baby or for me. He was fleeing his responsibilities. What a surprise!!! Why would I have ever believed that I would be with a responsible man? No, this is being lucky. I should know better that I don't have this kind of luck! I was mad at the world. I was mad at myself. I was mad at God that I felt kept letting me down. I was tired. I was losing my strengths, my ambitions, my dreams and my drive for life. How would I now face my life? I had no job, a boyfriend who did not want me and a baby to come. Why? Why do I need to face this now? I was mad at myself for being stupid enough to have believed in that man. I should have known. I felt this coming up and I just refused to open my eyes.

I spent the week-end alone brooding over my sorrow. On Monday, Antoine came back home as if nothing had happened. He talked about the wonderful weekend he had just spent with his kids (he had children from a previous marriage). Everything seemed to be fine for him.

"Good morning, Catherine!" he exclaimed. "How was your weekend?"

"How was my weekend?" I answered with rage. "Are you serious? Don't you know how I feel right now? I announce to you that I am pregnant and you leave right away. You don't even call me the whole weekend to see how I am doing? Who are you? You see, I think I don't know you at all. I have created a dream out of you and was not able to see you the way you really are. How can you treat me this way? Is that all I represent to you, a toy you play with for a while and you leave in a corner because it's just lost its interest?"

"Leave me alone" Antoine retorted. "I have more important things to worry about right now. I don't need this added to the rest. How could you have gotten pregnant anyway? You took the pill didn't you?

"Do you want me to show you how I got pregnant? Come here and I show you" I replied, ironically. "Yes I took the pill. I guess it did not work. There is a two percent chance to still get pregnant you know! The odds put me in that two percent".

"Catherine, you know we can't keep this baby. Please take it easy. Don't complicate my life more than it is right now. Go get an abortion!"

Antoine had just hacked me into thousand pieces. I could not believe what I had just heard. I had to sit down, dumbfounded by his words. The man I loved had just thrown me away in the abyss, totally insensitive to my feelings. I understood right then that he did not love me. He had never loved me. He just used me like he probably had used a lot of women. Just like a razor. He used it as long as the blades were new, sharp and shiny. As soon as they start losing their sharpness and shine, they don't work as well, you throw the razor away.

"Please leave me alone" I said. "Just go, I need to be by myself."

Antoine left without a word. I did not want to see him anymore. He even made me think about aborting my child. I was desperate and lost. How could I have this baby alone anyway? Look at me. What a failure I am. I have nothing, nothing.

It took me days of crying before I rose again to the sun. Nobody had the right to treat me this way. If I keep crying, he wins. This is the last thing I want. I have to be strong. I have to react and protect myself. I decided to go spend some time with my family, to talk to them and ask them for their advice. I needed an outlet. I needed someone to talk to, someone who would listen. My father who still lived alone opened his heart and allowed me to come and talk. One evening, my brother came with his wife. They saw how distraught I was.

"Jeff" I bellowed to my brother. I think I am going to have to abort. I can't face it. Antoine is right. This is just impossible. Look at me!"

A long silence followed. Then, his wife, Virginie, looked at me and said: "Stop destroying yourself, Catherine! You have to react. You have to create positive in your life. This is positive. A baby is life. Life is positive. Keep this baby and you will see your life changing in a positive way. It seems impossible to you right now because of all the wrong circumstances that are surrounding you, but you'll see, a few months from now, things will change. Parameters will evolve. You will be OK. Please have this baby. Do not destroy life. This is your chance. Now!"

Her words struck deep into my heart. She had shown extreme wisdom by expressing her thoughts. I did not know what to say. Finally, I said: "I never looked at this under this angle. Thank you for your support. I have to leave now".

So I left and drove back home not knowing anymore what was the right thing to do. I had made an appointment at the hospital to have the abortion a month away. What should I do? I went to bed and fell asleep.

When I woke up the next day, I felt amazingly calm and serene, accepting the situation I had put myself in and ready to face it as best as I could. I still was not sure what was the best thing to do so I decided to allow myself one month, one month during which I would observe myself, observe Antoine who was still coming once in a while visiting me. At the end of December, just before the new year, I would make a decision and would stick to it.

Antoine still had to travel a lot for his job. The only few times he was with me were without any fire, still like a calm lake. We were on our boat going nowhere, not happy together, fearing each other's company. When with me, he was distant, dreaming away, allowing his mind to be away from me, where he really wanted to be. I could feel his misery when he was around. He was suffering deeply and could not cope with himself and the situation. He wanted to hide. I felt the gap between us growing steadily and the only bridge that held us together was becoming narrower and narrower by the day. Antoine sometimes showed some compassion and tenderness by rubbing my stomach. However, he never mentioned anything about our future. He was still living in the past. He was vegetating in his present state. He was submitted to his life, overwhelmed by events.

The holiday season was upon us. Antoine wanted us to spend New Year's eve in a nice resort in the south of France. "We'll go there just to the of us, love" he mentioned. I made all reservations further to his request. I had organized everything and wanted to allow a glimpse of joy to invade my heart. May be we will be OK. May be he will accept things and be happy some day. May be I had to fight to reach this happiness and the right to be with him and his baby.

Christmas was over and Antoine was in the south of France with his children. Antoine was Jewish and did not celebrate Christmas. He had celebrated Passover with his family. We were supposed to meet at our resort 3 days before New Year's eve. Surprisingly, I had not heard from him for a few days now and started to worry. More exactly, I started to wonder whether he would make it for our few days together in our dream resort. What was happening again? I tried to ease my imagination, that was always very fertile. I was expecting everything. At least that's what I thought. Finally, one day before my supposed departure, the phone rings.

"Catherine, dear, how are you?" He always started his sentences this way. It generally meant that something was wrong. "I have something to tell you" Of course, I knew that. What's going on again?

"I don't think I am going to be able to make it for New Year's eve. I can't leave my children. They need me. I want to spend more time with them. I can have them the whole week, just for myself. I want to take advantage of this. Please forgive me. I won't spend New Year's eve with you. I just can't. My children are more important. And I told you, I don't think I am ready for what you want to offer me. I don't want another child". Here we were again. Another big punch right in my heart!

I felt like ripping the world, tearing out his eyes, kicking his legs, yelling so loud that my lungs would come out. I should have known. I should have known that something that good can't happen to me. I felt abandoned, one more time.

"I understand" I answered with a creaking voice. "You should have told me this long ago. You had made me believe and I was looking forward to being with you. I see how little I mean to you now. I am sorry. I am sorry I was not strong enough to accept the fact that you don't love me. I have been unable to look at reality as it hurts so much. It is much easier to hide it and create my own imaginary world, where you love me, you want me and your child with you, where you would take care of us. Oh well, at least, now I know. Have a good time! It is probably better if you don't call me anymore. I don't know that I want you around me. It is too painful. Good-bye".

I hung up the phone feeling all my hopes had been brushed away from the canvas of my life. I was devastated, desperate and angry. What would happen now? What was I going to do? I had to face reality and react, react and react again. I did not want to spend New Year's eve alone. I had to get out, think of something else. I could not spend my time crying and moaning on my fate. I called my friend Marie and asked her if I could come participate in the party that was organized by the city. I wanted to laugh and dance. I wanted to live.

Marie welcomed me and reserved an additional seat for me.

"We are going to have fun, you'll see!" she exclaimed, in an attempt to cheer me up.

December 31st finally arrives. 6 p.m. and I am getting ready to go out celebrate the New Year. I was going to wear a beautifu black evening dress. I would leave my hair long. I wanted to be beautiful. I wanted to feel beautiful. I was just grabbing my keys to jump into my car when the phone rang. It must be Marie, I thought.

"Hello" I answered, trying to hurry.

"Can I speak to Catherine?" I heard on the other line. It was a man's voice. An older man's voice. This is Mr. Gabay. Antoine's father." My heart started drumming as fast as the engine of a F-16 fighter. I had never met Antoine's father. Why would he call me on New Year's eve?

"Good-evening. If you don't mind, this conversation has to be short. I was up to leaving for my New Year's eve party. What is going on? Anything wrong?"

"Yes, something is wrong" he answered with a deep sadness in his voice. "I am in Bordeaux with my son. We are at the hospital. He tried to commit suicide. He swallowed two containers of sleeping pills. He is now recuperating as doctors just had his stomach pumped out and they think he'll be fine. He has been talking about you a lot and want to be with you now. Can I bring him to your home? Would you mind looking after him tonight?"

This was the straw that broke the camel's back. Not only did Antoine hurt me badly for rejecting me, now he tried to kill himself and ask for my help. Who am I here? A Guinea-pig? Who is he to show such disrespect? I am so tired of all this. However, I could not reject him now when he needs someone to help him. So I answered:

"I am so sorry to hear this. You must be devastated. Bring him home. I will be waiting for you. I will stay with him all night long but you'll have to find another solution after that. I am not a nurse and if he has reached that level of depression, he might start again. I would highly suggest that you ask for professional help. The sooner the better."

I felt responsible for part of Antoine's depression. I had to be here to help. Bordeaux was four hours away from where I lived. I had to wait until midnight for them to arrive. What a way to celebrate the New Year! I called Marie and explained the situation. She could not believe it. Actually, I could not either. I waited, minute after minute, hour after hour. Finally, they arrived. I greeted Antoine's father that I was meeting for the first time. Antoine was still staggered by the dose of medicine he had ingested. He looked very tired.

He fell into my arms, sobbing and crying. He said only thing to me "I want to die". He repeated these words non stop. "I want to die. I want to die. I want to die". I thanked his father for driving him to my place and told him I would call him again the next day. I tried to cheer him up by offering him gifts I had purchased for him, preparing dinner.

I encouraged him to go to bed and to try to sleep. I stayed awake all night for fear of seeing him do the same thing again. He sounded so desperate, so scared of living.

I had never seen anyone in that state of despair. I had never encountered anyone that had committed suicide. He explained that he could not face his life the way it was anymore, that it was too much and that he did not see any solution that would satisfy him. He could not start a life with me for fear of not being able to see his children anymore.

For Antoine, death was the only solution, the final escape to his misery and suffering. He had abandoned life. He was focused on himself, forgetting that the world around him was not so bad.

The next day, I drove him to a hospital two hours away from my home where his parents lived. His father had made sure that he would be looked after for at least a month. For two weeks after his suicide attempt, I drove morning and evening to and from the hospital, two hours back and forth, to spend as much time as possible with him. I drove in deep snow, taking risks on the frozen highways. I spent my days comforting him and listening to his torments. He sometimes would look at me. He would touch my tummy talking to the baby that he denied. He never thanked me for visiting him. When he had to introduce me to some other visitors, he did it with irony, almost laughing at who I was, totally disrespecting the fact that I was bearing his flesh. This made me feel so uncomfortable that I wanted to run, as far as I could away from him. His attitude towards me was eating away at me, hurting my pride, shutting the door to respect and happiness. I had done nothing wrong and yet I was treated like a thief.

This is something that my grandfathers always taught me. Always walk head up if you know that you are in the right. Never let anyone damage your pride. After these two weeks spent by his side in this cold hospital, I knew that I represented nothing to Antoine. He was not interested in my well-being. All that mattered was him. I was exhausted by these travels and by the energy he drew out of me. It was never enough. I never gave enough. Antoine was always dissatisfied and unhappy.

He finally left the hospital and looked a little better. He did not say anything about dying anymore. He was always highly sedated.

"It will be OK" he kept saying. "I will be OK". "We are going to look for a house and we will live together" he said.

I had a hard time believing in his words. I was not even sure that I wanted him by my side anymore. Sure thing, the next day, he was talking about dying again. All his words had no meaning. I could not trust him. He kept imagining the worst scenarios, trying to find out what would be the fastest way to put an end to everything and be successful this time. He kept saying that he only knows how to create misery in people's life. He is a loser, a bad person. He should go forever.

It took me these words to understand what my future would really be. I knew that I would not have him around. I had tried everything, had imagined everything, had given away all my energy to help him but nothing would do it. I had nothing more to give him and he did not want me around anyway. I made up my mind that I had to make decisions for my future by myself and that I would take full responsibility of my doings. I had to protect myself and protect the child I was carrying. I had decided to not abort. I will give birth to my child and raise him the best I can. I somehow knew things would turn out to be fine.

"I will love this child with all my strengths" I confided to Marie. "He will be my reason to be. He will become my life and my happiness. He will bring me joy and hope, strength and fulfillment. It will be a new life, a new beginning, new horizons. I will fight for him. I will cherish him, enlighten him, treasure him".

I had just announced to Antoine that I needed some positives in my life and that he could not and did not want to offer this to me. I explained that I had decided to keep the baby and that I would raise him by myself. I told him that I released him from his responsibilities, that he did not need to be around me anymore if he did not want to. I let him go. I set him free. I asked him not to contact me anymore and try to react to build his life again.

I had to erase this man from my memory. I had to accept

that my child would not have a father. I trusted my destiny and knew that someday, this suffering inside of me would go away, slowly but steadily. I was determined to find balance and happiness. I will be happy one day again. Soon.

So I did. I have spent the last twelve years of my life raising my daughter by myself. Her birth father has not been present. He still is not able to face her being on this earth and has chosen to ignore all that she is. It has been challenging but wonderful. Adelle is now sixteen years old and has grown to be an amazing young woman with average grades of 4.0, a place in high school sports dreaming to get a scholarship in softball and become a doctor.

I have absolutely not doubt that she will accomplish all of her dreams as she has the determination of a bull, the strength of a lion and the vision of an eagle. I have never stopped communicating with her despite our disagreements. I have always encouraged her to love herself deeply to make her believe that she can accomplish anything she wants because she can. Every day, I tell her how beautiful, smart and incredible she is as I know that these words are what is her essence and what unconsciously she believes in. I can't wait to see where she goes. I can't wait to share her adventures, her joys and her sorrows and continue to be the mother that she knows will always be here for her, no matter what.

DESPITE ALL THE HURT YOUR MAY FEEL IN YOUR HEART, ALWAYS TREASURE LIFE. IF YOU FIND YOURSELF PREGNANT WITH A MAN WHO DOES NOT WANT YOUR BABY, THINK OF YOUR- SELF AND PROTECT YOUR CHILD. DO ALL THAT YOU CAN TO RAISE YOUR CHILD WITH BEAUTY, FAITH AND DEEP, DEEP LOVE. A CHILD IS LIFE AND LIFE WILL BRING ABOUT POSITIVE. I KNOW HOW HARD IT IS BUT BELIEVE ME, THERE IS AL- WAYS A SHINING STAR IN THE DARKNESS OF THE NIGHT. POSITIVE ALWAYS ATTRACTS POSITIVE, SO BE POSITIVE! THIS IS THE LAW OF ATTRACTION.

"Believe that life is worth living and your belief will help create the fact
-William James

REALITY #5
GROWING PAINS

Growing up is hard. Growing is even harder. We experience it the first time in a very drastic way during out teenage years. I am sure you have your share of memories as a teenager. You hate the world, you hate yourself. Nothing makes sense. You parents are total idiots. You have the worse hair ever. etc. etc. etc. Nothing is right.

So now, what happens? Somehow, after a divorce, a death, a break-up or another traumatic event, you feel a little bit like that again. You hate yourself, you hate the world, you ex is the worse human being that you could possibly have met, and you have no clue as to who you are anymore.

Somehow you have to relearn everything. Your life's puzzle as you know it has been destroyed. Now you have to place each individual piece in different locations. They just don't fit where they used to anymore. During your married years, you thought you knew who you were. It may not have been completely perfect — you probably experienced some discomforts but you were in a familiar zone. You had your habits and even though happiness was not around the street corner every day, you could live your life pretty decently. It was not great but it was OK. You had put most of your dreams on the side as you thought they were unrealistic anyway. You gave up on a lot of your fantasies and your dreams. You were in what I call a state of "unconscious hypnosis".

Do you know that we constantly undergo hypnosis and become brain washed without having a chance to counteract? We so often believe unconditionally what we are told or what is presented to us. Radio spots, TV ads, billboards. We take them as truthful matters when in fact most of them are bare lies.

The truth is we can't blame ourself for such gullibility! Let's take a good look at ourselves and our society. As children, we have to follow the rules set up by our surroundings. These rules become our life and restrict our circle of observation, taking away all our natural tendencies. Although some do, it is extremely unlikely that, as a child of a young age —prior to the teenage years— we find the strength and the courage to rebel against adults. As a consequence, we fall into the belief system and are obligated to abide by it. With years, we slowly lose the sense of who we really are. We have become a piece of the puzzle and even if we don't love it, we accept it. It is what we know and feel comfortable with. How can we change when we become adults?

First, we have to realize that this is what happened and fully believe in it. Then, we have to find the strength to question it and challenge what we have been taught all our life. We have to question our whole belief system and rebuild a brand new one, more in accordance with what we believe we have become. I truly feel that if we had a way to expand an environment more opened to creativity to our children, we would allow them to get in touch with their inner self in a deeper way, while giving them the guidance they need to be able to grow in a healthy way.

As a teenager, I questioned everything. I always said "why does it have to be this way? Who believe is powerful enough to set such rules?" I never understood why I would be sanctioned for being too creative or for developing ideas that were seen as too extravagant. Looking at it now, I believe that extravagance is the substance of growth and discovery. Why should we sanction our children or young adults for being too extravagant? Why can't we let them express themselves in a more liberal way? The most incredible discoveries were made by extravagant people. They have been made by people who believed in the impossible; people who did not stick by the rules; people who had the guts to think outside the box and express it loud and clear.

The whole humanity is searching for the truth because unconsciously, we know that we have been living in lies for too long. I truly believe that there is no one truth. There are billions of truths. You just have to find the one that corresponds to who you are inside, well hidden within you. Only when we find what is deep inside of ourselves are we able to reach true happiness and be fully alive. This can be scary, as this discovery will probably change your whole world.

People around you will bear consequences of your change. You might see people leaving you and new ones coming into your life, who are more in sink with your soul and more in line with your purpose. You won't be the image of what other people wanted you to be, you will be the true you and you will find the people that can understand this true you. Your frustrations will diminish. You will finally accept yourself for who you are, because you will find total harmony between you and the outside world.

Please remember what I am up to telling you now: Stop abusing yourself and others will stop abusing you. Understand who you are and you will be understood and respected.

Others see you as you see yourself. Life is a mirror.

This process started with me after being married four years to my second husband. We did not have the same religion. He was Jewish, I was catholic.

February, 1995.

I was talking on the phone with my mother who had moved to Taipei, Taiwan for eight months following her husband who had been sent on a business mission. He was at a high level of an international Nuclear Plant Development company. They left in November of 1994. My mother was always ready to travel everywhere and discover new countries. She had not been in Taiwan before and that was a great opportunity for her. After three months there, she had already learnt some Chinese and seemed to be totally comfortable with her new environment.

"I love it here darling." She answered. "It is so different. Everything is new to me. It is very hot and humid. We live downtown Taipei in a sky scraper."

The population in Taipei is dense, as dense as pollution. People go out walking the streets with masks to avoid breathing the exhaust of the thousands scooters invading the streets like ants. Taiwanese people are hard workers, extreme negotiators and very welcoming. This is thanks to all these wonderful qualities that Taiwan has become such a successful country. It is the commerce center of the pacific. All goods coming from China transit there and are exported again all over the world.

"Why don't you come spend some time with us Cathy? You don't have anything that ties you to France right now. You are not working. This will be good for you" she said. "You need to see something else. You need to divert your thoughts to some positive in your life."

"I would love to come Mom" I answered starting to imagine my life there. "I feel so lonely here. So lost and scared right now. That would be wonderful to see you there. Can I really come? I can't afford it right now".

"Don't worry about this. I will pay for everything for you. Just relax and come. You need it more than you want to admit. This is an opportunity of a lifetime".

Being three months pregnant, I decided to leave for Taiwan. John, my first husband, with whom I stayed in good terms, drove me to the airport, wishing me good luck.

"I know I will learn a lot there" I told him. "Somehow I have a feeling that I am going to meet with my destiny. This trip is going to change the course of my life".

So, I left for Taiwan. After a 13-hour flight, the arrival in Taipei was quite something. I had never seen a country as dirty and unattractive as Taiwan. It was also my first real encounter with Asia. Taiwan is a big metropolitan country, with a population of 21 million inhabitants on a surface half of Nevada. The city of Taipei is surrounded by mountains which creates a natural basin where pollution clouds are stagnant. I also immediately noticed the numerous stray dogs running the streets, hardly able to walk, being hurt and handicapped. Most of them end up in a Taiwanese plate anyway. You never know if you eat chicken, cat or dog in Taiwan. It all tastes the same with a good seasoning sauce!!! It was raining and cold when I arrived. It was hard to believe I was right in the middle of the Pacific Ocean.

"How can you live here?" I kept asking my mother. "This is awful!"

"You get used to it" she kept answering. "There are some good things in Taiwan. This is a big international center. The world trade center in Taipei is huge, trading thousands of goods all over the world. Taiwanese people are incredible marketers. They have this in the blood. They like to negotiate. They want you to negotiate. If you buy something without negotiating, you lose a lot of interest and you are no fun. They in fact take it as an insult. It is part of the culture, part of their traditions."

This quickly became my favorite activity: running the streets of Taipei and negotiating with street vendors. I loved it and made incredible deals.

Two days after my arrival, amazed by this new environment into which I was evolving, my mother told me: " I am going to take you to a typical Chinese restaurant. I have never seen any foreigners there. They don't even speak English but the food is outstanding!"

It took me a while to get ready. I did not know what to wear. My pregnancy was hardly visible but I felt huge and unable to wear my normal clothes. I finally ended up borrowing a nice red outfit that belonged to my mother and that was quite charming. I think it enhanced my body while still dissimulating the little roundness around my waist. I felt beautiful while leaving the apartment. I felt happy and serene, ready to discover a new world, ready for a new life. I felt lucky to have such wonderful parents around me that would give anything to help and put a smile on my face. This gave me wings and courage again, courage to face my life and take full responsibility for it.

We went to the restaurant with one of my mothers' friends, Genevieve. Genevieve was full of spirit, a wonderful person. She laughed all the time. Both my mother and her made me feel so light, so happy. I started to see the light at the other end of the tunnel. I started to feel that there was a way to be happy. Despite my break up from Antoine, despite my pregnancy, despite the fact that I was alone, with no job in France, I knew I had my family and wonderful friends that would always cheer me up. I was now convinced that I was going to gain more energy and that everything would be fine.

We arrived in that typical Chinese restaurant after

walking the streets of Taipei for about ten minutes. The room was full of smoke, so crowded that we could hardly reach our table. The waitress sat us at our table and asked us in Chinese what we wanted. We looked at each other not knowing what to do as none of us spoke Chinese enough to be understood. So, my mother got up and went around all tables in the restaurant looking at what other guests had in their plates. There was no way we could explain to the waitress what we want in Chinese or no way we could understand what was on the menu. The only way to be understood was to do what my mother was doing. And she knew it. In three months, she had gained quite some experience dealing with the Chinese language, not knowing it. After looking at three or four tables, she reached a table where the people were not at all Chinese. They were American businessmen. And she started to talk to them.

"This is very clever what you are doing" commented one of them. They were delighted to help us choose our meals. When my mother came back, she told me "Cathy, there is a very good looking young man at this table". You've got to meet him!"

"Mother please" I said. "I am pregnant. Who would want a pregnant woman? Only someone totally insane or totally desperate!". We finally placed our order and were waiting for our food when that young man came to our table and started to talk to my mother again. He introduced himself. He was talking to my mother and Genevieve, not looking at me at all. I also did not want to look at him, feeling quite embarrassed and not knowing how to react in such an unusual setting. After talking about his life in the area, he said to my mother: "I currently live in Hong-Kong but have been looking around to eventually move to Taipei. I like it here. I just don't know the area too well yet!"

"Really?" my mother quickly responded. "I have been living here for three months now and have had plenty of time to visit the area. If you are interested, I can be your guide and show you around. Here is my card. Call me anytime."

She finally introduced me. He ended up almost forced to look at me. I also looked up at his face and crossed his light blue eyes for the first time. I shook his hand, introducing myself. I will remember this moment all my life. It was love at first sight. I knew I would spend some time with this man. This is the day I met Larry, my second husband.

We lived happily in Hong-Kong for a couple of years, where I moved right after giving birth to Adelle, my daughter. We then moved to the U.S. and moved several times where jobs would take us. We discovered differences that I had tried to put aside. After 4 years of forcing myself to believe that there were not important, I started to feel the need to be myself. The first need was to practice my own religion again, which I was not able to do, as he would not have understood that. He wanted me to change my beliefs.

One day, I told him that I needed to be myself again. I needed to get back to my belief system as I was losing track of my identity. I had voices at night telling me "go back to your religion Catherine" "You have to teach your daughter what you believe in".

This instantly created an immense gap between him and I. He did not understand why suddenly, I felt this need of going back to church and become more spiritual my very own way. Six months later we divorced. We could not combine both our needs as they were too different. The understanding and the maturity were not there. We could not carry our marriage the same way anymore. Because of my awakening and need of being who I really was, I changed my surrounding world. My world cleaned itself from all "impurities" that did not correspond to my inner self.

It has been twelve years now since my divorce and I now understand why it happened. I had forgotten who I was. I had put it aside thinking who I truly was was not so important. I was wrong. I am now living the life I want with my daughter and finding great peace in it. I live alone, spend a lot of time in meditation and have developed a better balance in my life. I am stronger, healthier and happier.

Any metamorphosis hurts. Any growth process will be painful, but once you reach the beautiful meadow at the top of the mountain and all the sweating part of climbing up heal is over, you feel relieved and proud. You have accomplished something. The world is open. What a relief! You will find joy and peace you never experienced before.

Is this happening to you? You feel like to need to grow but you do all you can to resist that process as it is so very scary. So here is what I'd like you to do:

1. Look at fear straight in the eyes and destroy it

Fear is what will stop you from going forward. The more your let fear invade you, the more you resist going forward, the longer the recovery process will be. You need to accept that you will be growing and therefore suffering for a while. But you also need to remember that it is worth it.

Our society is in complete denial. Everything is about suppression. We want to suppress pain by providing everyone with all the "anti" treatments. From antibiotics and anti-inflammatory to anti-depressants, we want to cover up our pains and instead of truly curing them, we suppress them so that, for a while, we won't have to deal with them.

This is the philosophy of allopathic medicine. We look at the symptom and we camouflage it. Allopathic medicine refers to "the broad category of medical practice that is sometimes called Western medicine, bio medicine, scientific medicine, or modern medicine". Allopathic medicine and allopathy —from Greek állos, other, different + páthos, suffering— are terms coined by Samuel Hahnemann, the founder of homeopathy. It meant "other than the disease" and it was intended, among other things, to point out how traditional doctors used methods that had nothing to do with the symptoms created by the disease and which, in Hahnemann's view, meant that these methods were harmful to the patients.

So, in other words, temporarily suppressing your symptoms is extremely harmful to your long-term health. You will feel better for a while but soon those symptoms will erupt stronger and stronger.

Imagine your fears made of several layers. Now, in comparison —as it will help you understand— let's look at layers in a volcano. In a cinder cone volcano, layers of ejected lava are combined with was is called "pyroclastic" layers, formed of "tephra": hot gas and rock that flow from the cone.

The classic volcanic cones are composed of several parts :

- Cone: the mound of ash and cinder
- Crater: the main opening, usually at the peak or summit
- Vents: openings from the cone
- Conduits: the lava channels connected to the vents
- Magma chamber: the underground source

of the liquid rock for the volcano. Imagine your fear being the bottom layer: the   magma chamber. Each time it becomes painful, you try to dismiss it by temporary killing it with medication as you don't want to deal with it. You suppress and suppress. Now ask yourself: What happens if the magma chamber of the volcano is constantly pushed back down to avoid it to come back up and let all hot gas and rock flow through the main cone. How long do you think the layers above the magma chamber will be able to sustain such pressure?

Certainly for a while, particularly if the upper layers (the medications) are strong enough. At one point however, the layers become more and more brittle as the pressure slowly creates cracks everywhere (the medication does not work as efficiently as your body is getting used to it). And one day, everything explodes to create the biggest eruption ever that no one survives.

Your body is like a volcano. The more you suppress or ignore the pains, the bigger the underlying pressure and one day "bang". The inevitable explosion (disease) occurs.

You know, it's interesting as yesterday, just before I was going to start writing this chapter, I had a message from my mother in France telling me that one of my cousins was found dead in her home, after committing suicide by hanging herself. Of course, huge shock.

She was 38 years old.

A beautiful woman with two beautiful children. She had been married for fifteen years and her husband had left her for another woman. They had been separated for about a year. I had heard through the grapevine that this separation had been very hard on her. I had also heard that her doctor had given her strong anti-depressant medications as from what he said, she was not able to fight on her own. As time passed, I was told that she needed stronger medications as she had attempted to kill herself twice.

So instead of finding other ways to help her deal with her pain, they suppressed it. Did they kill it? Absolutely not, they just suppressed it. Result? One day, the volcano erupted. Her magma chamber could not resist the pain anymore and it cracked.

She finally succeeded in putting and end to her suffering.

IF YOU ARE IN THE TYPE OF PAIN THAT FEELS UNBEARABLE, SEEK HELP FROM A VARIETY OF DOCTORS. HOMEOPATHS WILL TREAT YOU FROM A DIFFERENT PERSPECTIVE THAN ALLOPATHIC DOCTORS AND BOTH CAN BE COMPLEMENTARY TO EACH OTHER. DO NOT SUCCUMB TO THE PRESSURE OF OTHERS TRYING TO CONVINCE YOU TO DO EVERYTHING THE "STANDARD" WAY. STANDARD WAYS WORK FOR CERTAIN THINGS BUT IN SOME CASES, IT IS SMART TO LOOK AT ALTERNATIVES.

"Love is an essential vibration, the most powerful of the universe.
It is love that makes the suns turn, that grows trees and makes children
become adult - and love is eternal.
It is the same love that links two human beings.
It has always been and will always be.
Neither time, nor space, nor death will separate two people who were
linked by love"

Patrick Drouot

REALITY #6
LOVE, LOVE, LOVE

Love has different forms, different meanings. Love is hard to understand. I however took on a personal task to understand personal love to try to distinguish the various kinds of loves we experience. The love you feel for your spouse is very different from the love you feel for your children, your parents, or your friends. Love is a real puzzle.

Philosophers from the ancient Greeks have distinguished three notions that can be called "love": eros, agape and philia.

Eros means love in the sense of a passionate desire for an object, and is typically linked to sexual passion. Eros is the "love of desire". Eros is described as selfish and a response to the merits of the beloved, especially the beloved's goodness or beauty.

Agape is the sort of love that does not respond to the value of its object. It has come to mean the sort of love God has for us people, as well as our love for God and as an extension our love for each other. It is more a brotherly love. Agape is therefore more spontaneous and unmotivated and contrary to Eros, does not depend on reasons. Instead, Agape is supposed to create value in its object and initiate our fellowship with God.

Philia originally meant a kind of affectionate regard or friendly feeling towards not just one's friends but also towards family members, business partners, and one's country at large. Like Eros, Philia is typically understood to be responsive to good qualities in one's beloved. The main difference is the lack of sexual involvement.

Why am I telling you this? I believe it is critical to analyze and distinguish the types of love you experience. We so easily say "I fell in love with him" or "I'm head over hills for her". We must be very careful to not "fall" too quickly into one category until we truly know that our feeling is a legitimate one. Plus remember, "falling" in itself hurts.

I got into relationships too quickly thinking it was love. I had no doubt about it. I was so sure that within three months I was living with those persons. Then I looked back and wondered why those relationships didn't last. I realized the following: I did not know who I was dealing with. I had created an image that I wanted that person to be. It was a dream, pure imagination. I had built a hero in my mind. The problem with that is that dreams don't last forever. Reality falls on you pretty fast and when it did, my "star", my "hero" was no longer. I had in front of me someone I did not know, I did not admire and I really did not care for that much. The "love" I thought I had was no love. It was just infatuation. Just pure physical attraction that I translated into a feeling of love.

It is easy to make assumptions and that's wat I was doing repeatedly. We do it everyday because we think it is easier. We make assumptions about everything, about the way our partner thinks, about the way our boss is going to respond to our request, about what others think and do. We also make assumptions about what others think about us and get hurt because of them. We expand our imagination to a point that it becomes our reality. We then make a big deal and our whole world turns around lies that we have created for ourselves.

I was never able to find the right partner and I never understood why. I always kept blaming bad luck. I always felt unfortunate. Now I understand why. Everything makes so much sense. First of all, I always assumed things. I was never clear on anything, never confirmed things or feelings with my partners. I just assumed this is the way they felt, or this was why the reason they acted without validating with them their own judgments or opinions. I was always afraid to ask for clarification, fearing the answers. Making assumptions was easier. I believed in my assumptions so strongly that they became reality. I feared asking questions. I feared hearing answers.

This attitude led to one misunderstanding after the other; one disappointment after the other. Having a very fertile imagination did not help. I was creating my own world, without the awareness of whoever was sharing my world. I was therefore always disappointed.

I then refused to assume that others knew what I was thinking. I did not want to assume that my partner understood what I wanted. I realized how important it was for me to clearly state what my thoughts were. I needed to gain the maturity to be able to discuss my doubts, my questions, my insecurities. I always thought "how can't he understand that?" "he should be doing this without me telling him" "he should know better".

This kind of attitude leads to trouble. It became natural for me to act and think this way and I got lost in my vicious circle with no understanding on how to get out of it.

One of the biggest mistake is to make the assumption that you will change the people you are with, the people you "love". I've got news for you: you will not change them! These people will change only if they want to change.

Also, entering in a relationship with someone we want to change is dishonest. Then our relationship becomes with someone we've imagined, and anytime our partner steps outside of that imaginary projection, we will be disappointed. I now strive to be in an honest relationship, one in which we accept each other as whole individuals, and find a way to share our life experiences together.

I believe that in order for a relationship to be successful, you have to find someone who is real, true and genuine and you have to take the time to know him and then accept him for who he is. In order to be able to do so, you also have to know who you are and what your expectations and needs are, and express them loud and clear.

This was my problem. For a long time, I did not know who I was, therefore I never knew what my needs or expectations were and I never found a match to my personality. You have to be who you are, truly, without lie to find your match. Don't conform to someone's expectations just to please that someone. You will be able to fake for a while but one day, the true you will appear and this will open the door to misunderstandings and confusion.

With a clear understanding of who you are, you will create a clear communication with the people that surround you, be it at home or at work. This is I think the most difficult task to accomplish. I have been asking myself this question all my life and I believe I am finally starting to figure it out. How about you?

Speaking about love, remember my meeting my second

husband in that Taipei restaurant with my mother while I was pregnant? Well after she introduced me to him, he directed his eyes towards mine and I knew "love" was on the way. I looked up at his face and crossed his light blue eyes for the first time. I shook his hand, introducing myself. I will remember this moment all my life. It was love at first sight. I knew I would spend some time with this man. This is the day I met Larry, my future husband.

Spring 1995

"Did you notice how he looked at you, Catherine?" commented my mother's friend Genevieve. "I think something happened here. I think he likes you. And he is charming, don't you think so?".

"I agree" insisted my mother. "He is very charming and he keeps turning back trying to look at you. I think he is coming back."

They were right. Larry was back next to me and asked: "I am intrigued by something. How can women like you live in Taipei? What are you doing here?"

My mother explained that she had followed her husband who was in a mission and that I had come to visit for a few months.

"I understand" answered Larry.

"And what are you doing here?" I suddenly asked showing some interest and willing to participate more into the conversation.

"I represent a large American corporation for Asia Pacific. I am based in Hong-Kong but have to travel to Taiwan on a regular basis. I have been living in Asia for a year now." After a pause he suddenly asked: "I was thinking about a good day to go visit the area, since you nicely proposed and realized that I have some free time tomorrow. Would that work for you? I could meet with you somewhere around 10 a.m."

"10 a.m. is perfect!" replied my mother. "We can meet you at the ground floor of my apartment building. My address is on my card".

I couldn't believe what she had just said. We already had a date with this man that we had just met.

The next morning, Larry was right on time for our Taipei tour. It was a very hot day, a perfect one to take full advantage of the surrounding gardens and luxurious apartment buildings of the city. We visited two or three areas that we thought would be appropriate for him. He did not seem to focus too much on what we were showing. He was following us apparently enjoying the moment, more interesting to speak with me than anything else.

We ended up our tour in a superb villa where Genevieve

and her husband Charles were living. A residential quarter in the south of the city located in the middle of a lush tropical garden with a swimming pool, a fitness club and a high class restaurant. We decided to have dinner together and relax a little after hours of walking. Larry and I were listening to the general conversation others had. After a while however, we started talking to each other. I was attracted to him but at the same time had to remember that I was pregnant and that none of this seemed possible.

Yet, I kept dreaming. This is something I never stopped doing in my life. I somehow always naturally had a smiling moon floating above my mind that constantly allowed me to be positive and believe in the power of life and its miracles. Larry was in fact looking at me with wonder and tenderness. After dinner, we excused ourselves and went for a small walk in the flower garden. Flowers were incredible in Taiwan. The weather was most of the time warm and damp, which favored natural beauty all around .

Larry told me a little about his life in Hong-Kong and how he liked it there. Everything seemed so unnatural and unrealistic but somehow I knew that more was waiting for us at the corner of our lives. After a few minutes of walking, I felt he needed to know the truth about me, right then. I felt that our relationship would be more than just an acquaintance met in a restaurant.

There was not a single minute to waste. I could not live in the lie. So, I stopped and said: "There is something you need to know. I am already very attracted to you and this is not something I normally say to a man so quickly. You have to know who you are dealing with." I paused for a few seconds. Larry was looking at me with surprise. Then I continued:

"I am pregnant. I am three-month pregnant with the child of a man who does not want me. He was lost and suicidal and did not want any responsibility. I therefore decided to move on with my life and forget him. I could have had an abortion but the call of life was much stronger than the one of death. I therefore decided to assume everything on my own and I will have my baby." Dumbfounded by my declaration, Larry stopped and sat on a bench that was right next to him. "Sit down next to me" he said. "I don't know what is going on between us but I know something. No matter what happens, this does not change anything. I am sure you made the right decision. I am sure you did what you thought was best and I honor this. Thank you for your honesty. I appreciate it."

Tears came down my cheeks while I was listening to him. He seemed to be genuine. I believed him. "Thank you" I answered. "Thank you for your understanding."

Larry then looked at his watch and realized it was time for him to leave. He had to catch an evening flight to go back to Hong-Kong. He gave me his business card and went to say good-bye to my parents and their friends.

"Call me anytime Catherine" he said. "If you decide to come to Hong-Kong, please let me know and I will be your host".

I could not avoid thinking that I would never see this man again. How would anyone want a pregnant woman anyway? So I said good-bye with sorrow and went back to my parents.

"What a nice man" my mother commented.

"Very classy" added Genevieve.

"I know" I answered. "This can only be a dream".

Don't you think most people cross the same rivers? Nowadays, there is one divorce after the other. There is one family destroyed after the other. One of the reasons why this happens is that love has been misused and lightly taken. Love has been disrespected. When I talk about love, I first mean the love of oneself. If you and I had understood long ago that our self-love is the only condition to reach total happiness, we would not have gone through divorces. You have to love yourself before you can love anybody else. You have to know who you are before you can know anybody else. You have to deeply understand what you are made of before you can create a partnership of understanding, balance and growth.

We all dream about the perfect relationship. We all need love and warmth. We all look forward to having someone we can fully trust. If you are just now separated or divorced, try to use this coming year to build yourself, to understand who you are, to create your own happiness. Then, and then only, when you reach this inner happiness, will you be ready to share it with someone that is right for you.

BEING A SINGLE UNEMPLOYED EXPECTING MOTHER IS NOT THE END OF THE WORLD. I KNOW IT FEELS LIKE IT BUT IT'S NOT. YOU CAN MEET THE LOVE OF YOUR LIFE WHILE PREGRANT WITH THE CHILD OF ANOTHER MAN. IT CAN HAPPEN.

CIRCUMSTANCES HAPPEN.

STOP BLAMING YOURSELF. IT DOES NOT MAKE YOU A BAD PERSON. USE THE EXTRAORDINARY FACETS OF YOUR LIFE AND TURN THEM INTO SOMETHING POSITIVELY UNIQUE, SOMETHING INSPIRING FOR OTHERS. THIS IS YOUR GIFT. THIS IS YOUR LIFE. TREASURE IT.

God writes a lot of comedy... the trouble is, he's stuck with so many
bad actors who don't know how to play funny."
- Garrison Keillor

REALITY #7
THE MARRIED GUY ANTIDOTE

We all know from the very start that it is not right to have an affair with a married person. We are all aware of the wrong morals and of the hurt and damage such relationship can create. But sometimes, we fall into situations that we did not expect. We find ourselves in scenarios that have been rewritten to smitten us faster into a movie. We wanted to believe so much that we refused to see the signs and kept going with the script.

I knew all of this growing up but I also knew I had a tendency to believe what people told me. I had always been very gullible and always saw the world at my image: a good one.

So when I met someone new, I believed their words. I believed in their goodness and their righteous intentions. I never doubted that they were not acting properly and doing the right thing. You can say this is stupid or completely ignorant and you are right. But I was pure and I wanted to believe.

I grew up with a cheating father that had no problem switching women not too far from our eyesight. He had no problem coming back to my mother in the middle of the night after spending voluptuous times with his mistresses. I remember their arguments. I remember my mother's cries and I still feel her suffering when she knew he would go see them.

You know what they say? They say that we have a tendency to try to reproduce our childhood relationships. We seek for daddy in a man and we recreate exactly what we feared the most. Isn't that strange? Isn't that strange that this is exactly what happened to me. I hated my father for what he had done to us but I was unconsciously attracting the same kind of men: cheaters. I was unconsciously bringing to me what had hurt me the most. But at that time, I was unaware of it.

So what did I do? I put myself in situation that I could not get out of. Or it was too late for me to get out of.

Fall of 1993. Grenoble. France

"Good morning Charles! How are you? My god, how long has it been now? 5, 10 years? This is amazing! What a joy to see you again!"

I had just seen Charles again in the streets of Lyon, where I went to spend a day, trying to remember my time as a student. Charles had been my first love when I was 16. I was crazy about Charles. I had met him at a ball organized by the soccer association that my father was presiding. Charles had invited me to dance. I had succumbed to his charm.

At the time, Charles was working for my father and my father refused that I see him. "You can't see someone like this Catherine!" he kept saying. "He is not like us. He does not come from the same social level. I do not want you to see him and there is no discussion!"

Charles came from Portugal from a very modest family. It was not acceptable for a girl like me to see him! Nonsense. My fathers' words never prevented me from seeing Charles and being in his arm dreaming about life together. I loved his dark hair and dark eyes that knew how to reach deep in my heart. With Charles, I had always been on a cloud, unable to see reality. The only reality that I was interested in was the one of his smile, his laugh, his embraces. I was charmed. It was with Charles that I discovered the pleasures of the skin. I loved him and would have given him anything.

I finally left him when leaving for the United States. I was going to be a world traveler and he had no plan on doing the same thing. I concluded that I had to move on and forget him. My father was probably right. We are too different. Since that day, I had not seen him again.

Charles was now married with two children. His life

seemed to be well ordered. He looked happy.

"Catherine" he exclaimed "I can't believe it's you! You have not changed!. This is still you, my little Cat! Why did I let you go? What a fool I was! You, my muse, my forever dream!"

"Oh, come on Charles" I answered with sarcasm. "Don't give me this crap! What is going on with you?" I asked him thousands of questions. I wanted to know everything about the only man I believed I had really loved.

Charles told me about his life, about his wife and children and about the new job he just got. He had just started to work for an international trading company in Lyon that was extremely successful. He seemed to have found his way and was thrilled with his new endeavor.

"How about you darling? What are you doing now?"

I had to tell him about my layoff and disappointments, about my divorce and my sorrow." I had a wonderful job for two years Charles but I was just let go as the owner wanted to put his son at my position and that there was no place for me anymore. I was devastated for a while but I start to find the strength to react again and look around for opportunities. I have been navigating on tumultuous rivers towards unknown destinations. I am now on flight 0000 towards no man's land. I don't recommend it by the way Charles! I don't have any job and I don't have any love anymore. This is a new me, a new beginning and I have to look at opportunities. I keep believing something will come up soon. I have everything to rebuild and my soul strong to carry on this task.

"I am not worried for you" answered Charles. "You have the strength of a bull and the determination of an eagle. You have everything to succeed honey and you will, wherever you are. I believe in you and remember, I am the expert. I will also be here to help you. I know a lot of people and I will keep my ears open."

"All right. I accept your help" I retorted. "I accept with pleasure and relief as I need a little compassion and warmth, I admit. Here is my phone number. Call me any time. Don't forget, I am very mobile. I am ready to go anywhere in the world. Nothing keeps me here"

"No problem" replied Charles. "I will think about you and contact you soon. In the meantime, take care of yourself, be strong!"

I hugged Charles and said goodbye, a smile on my face. I was thrilled to have found him again.

And a few months later:

"I can't take it anymore Antoine! Leave me alone! Our story is leading nowhere. Forget me, go back to your wife where you belong." I cried on the phone while desperately trying to push away the man that I had deeply fallen in love with. I was then in the south of France, spending some vacation time with my parents that had rented an apartment on the French Riviera.

Summer 1994, year of my 30th birthday.

A year before, I had met Antoine through Charles. Antoine was Charles's boss and as Charles promised, he helped me. He introduced me to Antoine who was looking for help for his international markets. Antoine had contacted me right away. I totally matched the profile he was looking for. He had proposed that I work for him as a consultant for his European markets. I had accepted the offer, needing a job and being very interested in the prospect. I had survived my desperation. Thanks to him, I was back into the business world.

I immediately connected with Antoine and loved his professionalism. He was strong minded, organized and a man of decision. He believed in positivism and knew how to communicate it to his surroundings. He was born a leader. People around him wanted to succeed and make him happy. He was of a rare intelligence, very sharp with numbers and a high-end negotiator. I was very impressed and wanted to become like him and learn from him.

He had created a company that was selling materials to create signs and had traveled the world to find competitive countries where to purchase these products. He was juggling with foreign languages like a clown juggle with balls. He had also become an expert at investing. He seemed to know everything, and to fear nothing. I had dreamt of meeting a man like him. I thought this would not exist in fact. He was a mentor for me. I was learning so much from him. He took me everywhere he went. I participated in all kinds of negotiations by his side. I had become his right hand, working at growing his business.

We traveled to many different countries together. We had spent a lot of time together alone and had many occasions to know each other better. We had become accomplices in everything. We just needed to look at each other to understand what was going on and were able to negotiate the best deals together.

One of our trips took place in Spain where we had to visit a few agents of ours and communicate a new incentive program. We had decided to drive to Madrid for a 4-day trip. Antoine had planned to let me manage the whole thing, knowing I was now ready to play a more important role in the company. He just wanted to be present and observe. These four days were exhausting as we never went to bed before 1 a.m.. In Spain, people start their day around 9 a.m., take a small nap after lunch and don't have dinner until 11 p.m. or midnight.

This time schedule was killing me. I am not a night owl and had to fight to stay awake that long. We had done a tremendous work together and were ready to head back to France. That night on the 4th and final day of our trip, we were leaving after a dinner at 1 a.m.. The decision was to be made to either spend the night in a local hotel or drive back home. I was exhausted and wanted just one thing, sleep. That was not the case of Antoine. He wanted to go home. We drove the car towards a long journey back home at one in the morning.

Antoine had been married for seven years and had two boys whom he loved dearly. He had confessed to me that he was not happy in his marriage anymore and that he and his wife were living separately for a while. He mentioned not having too much in common with his wife anymore. Antoine came from a Jewish family and had been raised as such. Family was very important to him. It was his balance. He also confessed not being too faithful to his wife, having adventures here and there. I started to wonder why he was confessing so much to me. I had always looked at him as a work partner, nothing else. I always had refused having any personal relationships with people I was working with and this was going to be the case with Antoine too, at least this is what I tried to convince myself about. Nothing should have put us together. We came from two different worlds. I am a catholic, he was Jewish. Jewish people in France are still put aside and don't mingle too much with other people. There is still this reluctance and prejudices against them. "They are not like us!" my family always said.

Antoine knew that I was available, divorced and not

dating. This trip back to France was the strangest thing that ever happened to me. At 3 a.m., while driving on a desert highway, I was half asleep not too sure about where I was and what was happening. We were listening to a romantic music and the ambiance started to warm up. I felt Antoine's eyes on my body but did not make a move fearing everything at that moment. Suddenly an emotion, a drive was floating around in the small containment of the car, surrounding our hearts and our heads. Antoine's hand frivolously glided towards mine and ended up caressing it with deep passion. It was a unique moment in time where our hands were melting in a warm dance. I remember the movement of our fingers playing with each other, in a loving dance. He then brought my hand to his lips and started to kiss me. I did nothing to resist. I had no strength to resist. It was a unique moment in time, a delightful tango that I could not stop.

We were alone in the deep darkness of the night. He stopped the car and brought me into his arms with passion. After this futile moment in space, we started driving again, both drunken by what had just happened. On a cloud, we refused to allow ourselves to think. We did not want to know if what we were doing was good or bad. It just was. We arrived in my home town around 5 a.m.. Antoine had to leave me home to head to his office.

"Are we going to see each other again?" he asked.

"I don't know" I answered. "I never went out with married men and look at me now. What am I doing? I must have lost my mind. This is not good. This is going to be complicated and bring us more problems than joy. I don't know. I don't know. I will call you. Have a good day!"

Antoine turned his car around and left. I felt totally abandoned and lost. I felt empty like a dry lake, not having enough tears to express my disarray. I knew that I was already falling in love with him, this Jewish guy that was my boss and that I always said I would not touch. But, somehow, I had seen him again and again, and again. It was like an addiction. We met in hotels to share this incredible passion that was ours. We share these intense moments of happiness and tenderness.

I had never experienced anything like this before. We only saw each other sporadically on evenings during the week. I painfully learnt what was the life of those lonely mistresses, sharing love moments with these married men who desperately tried to live a normal life. Antoine never said that he would leave his wife for good and I never asked him to. I was accepting having him like this and thought I would enjoy this as long as possible. I knew that one day it would end. For now, it was good the way it was. We were lovers, hiding everywhere we went. We would probably remain like this as long as time would allow us.

We spent one year just like this, like fugitives on an endless road, stealing these moments of time that kept us alive. How long would this fantasy last? Was it important anyway? I didn't want to know. I started however to wonder where I was going. Where would this lead me? Am I building anything or am I just faking life? Is this what I want to be: a mistress that a man hides living in a lie? This answer was obvious. It was no, no and no again. I spent most of the time alone, wondering what he was doing and where he was. Very quickly, I couldn't stand this relationship. I wanted to live in the open world. I wanted to be recognized and proud of who I was. I wanted Antoine for myself and just for myself. I didn't want to share him anymore. But did I have the right to ask for something like that? He was married after all.

So, lost in my selfishness, one day I asked Antoine to make a choice. It was either leaving his wife for good or leaving me for good. I didn't accept this cheating nonsense anymore. Now I wonder how I ever accepted it. Antoine didn't know what he wanted. He wanted everything. This arrangement was perfect for him. He had his family on one side and a lover on the other. What a perfect combination most men love to have! Antoine was afraid of time. He couldn't bear getting older and living the life of an adolescent again and again was somehow comforting to him. He was in constant search of his inner self, insecure and scared. He was one of this men looking like men but being in fact big children in a man's shell, playing the seduction game to prove themselves. He had a need to seduce that was never appeased.

The more time passed, the more betrayed I felt and

Antoine refused to answer my questions. He was neglecting my requests, avoiding my concerns. I started to bother him, to disturb his little routine. He could not face reality but did not want to leave me either. He wanted everything, always. He was the center of the earth and wanted to remain so. Everybody around him had to be submitted to his will, like a slave.

"You can't leave me!" threatened Antoine on the other side of the phone line. "You will never love anybody like you love me. You will never share anything as powerful as what we have. Don't make that mistake, please! I have you under my skin."

I had to put an end to the conversation. I could not take his words anymore and I was in deep suffering. I had to terminate this relationship that was going nowhere and the phone was the easiest way to do it. I could have never looked at Antoine in the eyes and tell him what I was saying. I had to forget him and turn the page to a new chapter of my life. Antoine had destabilized me. I had become weakened by the feelings I had for him. During this time with him, I had to forget about myself to satisfy his needs. He had taken advantage of it. Now I felt degraded and unworthy. This had to stop.

"Is this really what love is? Is love synonymous of suffering? Do we have to cry to be able to live with the one we love?". All these questions haunted my mind. Of course, I had no answer. Was this the price of happiness? In Saumane, in the south of France near Avignon, I was visiting my parents. I needed to find some peace and be in a quiet environment far from everything. Antoine had to get out of my life. I had decided not to talk to him anymore.

My mother was a great help in motivating me to forget him and blowing away all these torments of mine. I had to start smiling to the world again. My sky was now darkened by heavy clouds ready to pour rain on a dry land, the land of my hurt heart. The storm was gone, shaking the last ramparts that were protecting my life, and the love that was still alive within. Lightning had fallen and lightened up the landscape of my future.

Soon, after the wind and the rains, the sun would shine through again. I had to move on and smile to life. I had to keep believing in love, again.

NEVER GO OUT WITH A MARRIED MAN. 99.9% OF THE TIME, IT WILL LEAD TO DISASTER, TO LIES AND TO A TOTAL LACK OF BALANCE. YOU WILL LOSE YOURSELF IN A FAKE WORLD AND IT WILL TAKE YOU A LONG TIME TO RECOVER. THESE MEN FIND THOUSANDS OF REASONS WHY YOU SHOULD BE WITH THEM. IGNORE EVERY ONE OF THEM. KNOW THAT YOU WILL ALWAYS BE THE FIFTH WHEEL AND THAT YOU WILL ALWAYS BE TREATED AS SUCH. MOST OF THE TIME, THESE MEN ARE WEAK, EMOTIONALLY UNSTABLE AND HAVE BECOME PROFESSIONAL LIARS AND FAKERS. THEY CAN'T EVEN RECOGNIZE TRUTHS FROM LIES AND HAVE CONVINCED THEMSELVES THAT THEY ARE ONLY "VICTIMS" OF THEIR CIRCUMSTANCES. DO NOT LISTEN. RESPECT YOURSELF AND BE PROUD OF WHO YOU ARE AND OF WHAT YOU STAND FOR. ALWAYS!

It's not that I'm so smart, it's just that I stay with problems longer.
- Albert Einstein

REALITY #8
WORK, MONEY & MLMS

Summer 1992

I am attending a meeting organized by a multi-level marketing company. Some of its members invited me, promising that I would make huge amounts of money if I became a member. This is how I met Don. Don was one of the top level sales people in the organization and was leading the meeting to motivate his peers.

Don was a tall handsome dark hair man and carried this innocent look with him that attracted my eyes. He was working with his father in his accounting firm. He seemed to know everything about this multi-level marketing organization and was extremely convincing while exposing the various facets of the business. I got interested in joining as a member and had nothing to lose. I wanted to develop my own business and this seemed to be one way to do it without investing huge amounts of money. So I became an avid follower and participated in all possible meetings to start selling and developing a regional market.

Don noticed my interest and my spirit for success and

expressed his support whenever I needed it. I found some kind of comfort in him. I also found a friend in him.

The principle of what they also call "Network marketing" is the taking in charge of one's own enterprise based on the self-development and personal blossoming. They all marketed this new trend with the fact that it is supposed to "transform your whole life by making it a suite of success stories that improve your existence forever". Well, did I believe in this! This network attracted hundreds of believers due to the high unemployment rate that was dominating the French market (interesting how we are going through the exact same thing this year in the US). Everybody was ready to believe in miracles! They praised individual leadership skills improvement thanks to the acquisition of some unique knowledge that plays a determining role into reaching financial freedom. And I could go on and on describing what I now understand as the biggest business trap in history. But at the time, I believed in it, invested in it and lost a lot.

I thought I had the perfect profile of the type of people they were looking for. Of course, I was willing to invest money. This is probably what ranked me into the "perfect profile" category. I was ready to become "great" and "the best of all". This in fact motivated me and gave me again the energy to dream about success. Despite the fact that I was not sure what I was doing and where I was going, I found in this project a lot of pleasure and motivation.

After a few weeks of work with Don, who by the way made more and more money thanks to all the people who had decided to invest on his project, I realized I was going nowhere. I had purchased the equivalent of what is now $4,000 and had not sold 10% of my products. Nobody wanted them! I also quickly understood that the only people who really make money in this kind of business are the one on the top of the ladder who were at the beginning of it. I had fallen in the trap of the weak ones. I had been the pray of a stratagem and decided to abandon all of it, put my dreams on the side and focus on something more realistic. I was mad though. I could not bear seeing these people attracting other people with very little money and have them invest it all in their buffoonery. I was mad at Don for doing this and started to fight against it. I was mad at him trying to make me believe in this lie. He had become so greedy with money that he had forgotten what he was really doing. And so I discovered something I would have never imagined.

"Be realistic, Don" I complained. "Look at what you are doing. You are just taking advantage of so many people! Is that how you want to grow in society? Is that how you want to build your wealth? You should be ashamed of yourself. This is disgusting." Don first looked at me with a grim and was not sure what to think. After a few days of not talking to me, he then came back and responded "You are right Catherine. I was out of reality. This is not what I want to do. I never wanted to do this in fact. I have been trapped in this and did not realize what

I was doing anymore. I am sorry. I will get out of it right away to focus on better avenues".

I was of course thrilled with Don's decision and quite proud of myself for convincing him to quit. All this brought us close to each other. We had become great friends. I felt this irresistible attraction for Don but was not sure whether it was him or me just dreaming about being in love again. Was I falling in love with him or just with the idea of being in love again? I was surprised to be able to forget about the love I felt for Antoine so easily. Was this real? Again, I was swimming in an ocean of unanswered questions, slapped in the face by regular waves that made me sometimes remember this state might just have been part of a substitution process, in the attempt to forget Antoine. I didn't know. I now realize all the love I had for Antoine was transferred to Don and that my apparent happiness was just a rewinding movie scene that would stop soon.

Don visited me regularly. We were in the middle of August and the heat was forcing everyone to spend some time in the mountains at higher altitudes whenever possible. Don and I spent a lot of time hiking in the beautiful forests of the Alps that were standing proud surrounding the city of Grenoble. Everything seemed simple again. I was soothed by Don's presence. I felt happy next to him.

We shared many wonderful moments together as friends. One day, two months after we first met, Don came to visit me and took me for a walk. He suddenly stopped and looked at me deep in the eyes:

"Catherine, would you like to spend some time with me?"

"Of course" I answered. "I love to spend some time with you. You know that".

"No, I mean, would you like to spend some time with me as a... couple. I want you by my side. I am falling in love with you. I want to work with you, live with you, travel with you. Do you understand?"

I couldn't say a word. I stayed a few minutes that felt like hours in total silence just staring at him. "Do you really mean what you say?" I finally asked.

"Of course I do. You are the most wonderful woman I have ever met. I want you with me".

" I don't know, Don" I added. "I don't know. Give me some time to think about this. I am still swimming in the ecstasy of doubt. I don't know if I am still in love with Antoine or not. I am so confused right now. Please give me some time"

Don left in disarray. He told me he was heading towards church to pray. He wanted to ask God's help. After a couple of hours, he came back knocking at my door again.

"Catherine, listen, let's spend a week vacation together.

Just the two of us. I would like to take you to Normandy in a beautiful spa resort. You are tired. You need some rest and so do I. Please accept. This will give us a chance to know each other better. It will help us look at things more realistically".

I looked at him with a doubt but finally accepted. After all, he was right. I was exhausted. A change of landscape could only be good for me.

So, we left. One day later we were on the train that took us to Normandy. We were going to spend a whole week in a spa on one of the most beautiful beaches of Northern France. We took a late night train to Quiberon. We had a cabin with two bunk beds. It was midnight when Don and I were still talking to each other. We were talking about life, about love, about everything that a man and a woman can talk about in the middle of the night. This is when we were ready to fall asleep that Don reached for my hand from the upper bed. I did not know what to do. Don and I were friends and I was not sure if I wanted more than just be friends. My heart started beating faster and faster, frightened by the idea of starting a romance with him. My hand finally moved towards his. The warmth of his skin became overwhelming. This hand communication lasted a few seconds. Not a word was said.. Don brought his hand back up and we both fell asleep in the magical moment of the night, with the background sound of the train.

We finally reached Quiberon and arrived at the hotel early morning when sea gulls were just waking up flying low on the horizon. We could smell the odor of fresh caught fish and enjoy the scenery of fishing boats coming back from their early morning trips. The hotel was right on the beach surrounded by two big cliffs that were dominating the bay. We were taken to the room that we would share, overhanging the incredible ocean view that delighted our eyes and senses. The facility offered tens of various spa treatments, one more luxurious than the other. We both enjoyed as many treatments as possible, forgetting everything, living in the present moment.

We were happy and relaxed sitting on the lounge chairs of our balcony when Don looked at me very seriously and said: "I have to tell you something."

The sound of his voice worried me. I quickly replied: "What happened? You look extremely serious and sad. Are you going to tell me that you are married, or that you are sick, or what, what Don, what is it?"

"I have something very hard to tell you and I need to do it now as I can't continue looking into your eyes without telling you everything about me".

At this point, I was really worried. What else was waiting for me? It is always like that. I soon as I start enjoying life and a glimpse of happiness with a man, something bad happens. What was it now with Don?

"You are scaring me Don. I am feeling terrible suddenly!"

"Please just listen to me Catherine. Let me talk. Once I am done you are free to do whatever you want. You can leave right away or you can stay and give me a chance. I am having a wonderful time with you and I want to hold you in my arms and become your lover. However, in a few minutes, the future will be in your hands. I feel so happy now but also know that I don't have the right to this happiness." I was now carefully listening, looking more and more upset.

"I did something very wrong two years ago. I committed a crime that is reprehensible by law, but I am still a free man as no one knows about it. At that time, I was living with a woman who was going through a lot or hardship in her life. Her husband was mistreating her and her 4-year old little girl. She then left him to come live with me. I decided to help her out as she seemed scared and could not live with him anymore. We started a love relationship that became worse by the day. Her husband threatened to kill her and her daughter. He was a drug dealer. He was very dangerous. I tried to intimidate him by returning the threats back but nothing did it. Elaine was devastated. I had to do something to save her and protect her little girl. I was so convinced that she was in danger, and I guess I felt I had to be her hero, her savior. Life just could not continue like this."

"So, what happened?" I anxiously asked.

"Catherine, I ..." Don paused for a few seconds, having obviously a hard time letting the words out. "I committed a murder. I hired two gangsters to kill him. I am a murderer!"

I suddenly felt like the sky was falling on me. I had expected everything but this. I was never in my life in this kind of context, speaking with a murderer about his murder. I felt out of space, scared to death with the one and only need to run away as fast as I could. I tried to stay calm and down to earth, staring at Don without a word, realizing that I did not know that man. I was in a hotel room with someone who had killed someone else. I believe my face must have turned pale as Don asked me if I was feeling OK. I felt like throwing up and yelling at the same time. Don had this innocent look. I thought he was so straight and honest and reliable and safe. I was going to start a romance with a... MURDERER!

I looked at Don and excused myself. "I need to be alone for a while Don. I don't feel very good. I just need to be alone. I can't believe what you just said to me. I'll be back soon".

Don let me go without saying a word. I went on the beach where I sat down and stared at the ocean waves for a couple of hours. I felt lost and was desperate for help. I was totally stunned by this news. How could he do this? Don, not Don!. Can I believe him? Is he trying to create stories and play with me? I started to wonder what I did to the world to deserve this. Why do I always have to be with disturbed people? Am I attracting them all?

Thousands of questions came to my mind and I could not find one single answer. I was now in a world that I had never known and that did not fit me. I never had to deal with justice or the police before and I knew somehow that if I remained silent, I might have become accomplice. I was not sure of anything anymore. How can I go back to this hotel room where Don was probably still waiting? That room had now turned into the anti-chamber of hell. I was panicking.

I finally returned to the room. Don was waiting for me in the same position that I left him. He looked scared.

"I have been thinking Don" I said "I am sorry. I can't stay here. This is not me. This is not my world. I would be haunted by what you have done day and night. What is my role now as a honest citizen? What is my responsibility? You have shared something with me that make me your accomplice if I don't say anything. Why? Why are you doing this to me? You have some responsibility here Don. You have to give yourself to justice. You can't continue living as if nothing happened."

Don understood. I packed my things and left. He came back a few days later. Don had confided that he knew nobody could know about what he did. However, I started to wonder. He had told me the truth. He might have told the same thing to other people and one day, the police would know too. Don was so haunted by what he did that he could not face it alone. He had to share it.

"I am now going to spend the rest of my life making up for what I did." He added. "I am going to help people in need. I know that if I do this, God will forgive me and allow me to live a normal life. I did what I did to protect a woman and her child. God knows I did not have any choice. It was her and her child or him."

"Don" I replied. "There is always a choice. My choice is life. There is a justice department in this country that deals with cases like this all the time. This is not your role to decide whether or not someone has to live. I totally disagree with that statement."

Don was obviously lost and tried to find some comfort in the horrible thing he had done. I know that I was not going to be able to bring him the comfort he was looking for. The whole thing was not right. What was I going to do next? Did I have to go and denounce him to the police? Was I going to remain silent? I did not know what to do. I was scared.

A couple of weeks later, my father received a phone call from the police department. They wanted to talk to me. Don had given himself up and had mentioned my name. He mentioned he had told me everything. They came and asked me details of what I knew. I gave them all. They mentioned that they had found the man's body buried at the top of a mountain. They also mentioned that I had nothing to worry about. They just wanted to confirm all that Don had told them.

This was an experience I hope to never live again. It again taught me that time is the essence. It is critical to take the time to know someone before getting involved deeply as when you are too deep, it is much harder to get out of the trails. Then, often, money is involved as you have started to share financial responsibilities and when finances are mixed, it adds another level of complication to the deal. Take your time. Be patient and learn slowly to observe before you commit.

Coming back to MLMs, I experienced the ride again this year, in Reno, Nevada. (I don't learn anything, do I?). I was unemployed and desperate and approached by a "friend" who told me he had the "opportunity of a life-time". At first, I pushed him away and then, because of his persistence, I gave in and signed up thinking that after all there is no gain with no risk. I started attending the meetings and quickly fell into the brainwashing pool that they all had carefully set up every week. I believed that in order to succeed, I had to spend a minimum amount of money in products. I also believed enough to try to bring other people in the system but I was not very good at that. By the way, I apologize to all of you that I tried to enroll into the system. I made a mistake. I quickly understood why I could not bring results: I just did not feel right about whom I had become and could not sell something I doubted.

So the experience quickly stopped. It was hard to get

out of the herd as the herd leaders do all they can to keep you in their clan. But I did and never regretted it as I now know that only a very small percentage of people make it in this business. It is a business that flourishes in times of economic hardship. It grows like weeds when the soil is made of unstable and hurt grounds. MLM marketing materials reveal that much of the message is fear-driven and based upon deception about income potential. Watch and be careful before making the decision to get in Multi-Level Marketing. Know that you are dealing with people that have become experts in human psychology and will know which words to use to attract you like a bee to honey. Then they keep the beehive warm and as closed as possible so that you lose track of reality. It is a world that fools you if you are weak enough to be manipulated. Just watch and analyze carefully before you get in any of those. And if you are willing and ready to exploit friends and family for personal gain, go for it!

But before you make the decision, please read articles on this website: www.mlm-thetruth.com.

Here are some facts:

- In the largest of all MLMs, Amway, only half of one percent of all distributors make it to the basic level of "direct" distributor, and the average income of all Amway distributors is about $40 a month

- In 1998, NuSkin paid out 2/3rds of its entire rebates

to just 200 upliners out of more than 63,000 "active" distributors. The money they received came directly from the unprofitably investments of the 99.7% of the others.

- MLM's almost always lead to a loss for new recruits. The founders and a few are at the top of their pyramids of participants are enriched at the expense of a multitude of down line participants, approximately 99% of whom lose money.

- MLM's typically bleed new recruits of their funds by inducing them to buy products on a subscription basis, to pay for ongoing training, and otherwise draining them of their resources until they run out of money or give up.

- MLM products must be priced high enough to support a huge network of distributors. Prices are rarely competitive with alternative retail outlets. MLM products are sold to recruits to "do the business," rather than to persons outside the network of participants.

- To profit at a recruiting MLM, you would need to work long hours and be willing to constantly recruit to replace drop outs. You also have to be willing to deceive large numbers of recruits into believing it is a legitimate income opportunity. These people seldom profit, but are instead only fattening their up line's commission checks and enriching founders.

- You will be stuck to your phone and to meeting the

qualifications for commissions and bonuses. You will received constant pressure to recruit new participants. If you don't, they'll tell you that you have a problem and that you need to "evolve" spiritually to become successful.

- The system itself dooms almost all participants to failure. MLM is built on an endless chain of recruitment of participants as primary customers. It assumes both infinite markets and virgin markets, neither of which exist. It is therefore inherently flawed, fraudulent, and profitable only for founders and those at or near the top of their respective pyramids of participants. Despite hard work and their best efforts, the vast majority will always lose money.

DON'T LET YOURSELF BE SOLD BY THE TYPICAL CATCHWORDS USED BY MULTI-LEVEL MARKETING COMPANIES. SOME OF THOSE WORDS ARE:

- MORE TIME TO LIVE
- FREEDOM
- TRAVEL THE WORLD TO BEAUTIFUL RESORTS
- RETIRE SOON
- MILLIONS OF DOLLARS
- WAKE UP WHEN YOU WANT
- BE PART OF A FAMILY THAT WILL ALWAYS BE HERE FOR YOU

REMEMBER THAT MOST MLM LEADERS ARE VICTIMS OF THEIR OWN DECEPTION AND END UP BEING FORCED TO JUSTIFY THEIR FLAWED PROGRAMS. YOU WILL BE SOLD A DREAM THAT VERY FEW ACHIEVE. INVESTIGATE AND KNOW WHAT YOU ARE GETTING IN BEFORE YOU DO.

"Defeat is not the worst of failures.
Not to have tried is the true failure."
- George Edward Woodberry

REALITY #9
DEALING WITH STRESS AND TAKING RISKS

Stress is part of life. It can either weaken you or make you stronger. Which one do you choose?

I'm asking you because it's a choice. It's a conscious decision you need to make and remind yourself every single day. The energies of the universe will challenge you, testing your resilience. Most people give in to the stress vibes and end up in states of despair. Some even die. But listen to this very carefully: if you can consciously look at stress face to face and decide that you are stronger than its powers, you will go through the clouds of doubts. You will realize how capable you are. You will feel powers you didn't know you had and you will walk head high towards the sun, believing more than ever in yourself, in the world and in what you can and will do to make a difference. As it is your belief that will move heaviest rocks. It is your faith that will bring life to your own truths. And it is your own truths that will inspire others to do the same. It is together that we can make this world a better, happier and safer place.

The most stressful time of my life was when I realized I had no choice but closing my business after three years of working night and day to build it up. I always had the dream of becoming an entrepreneur. I always wanted to have my own business, grow it, hire great people and make a positive difference by offering new products and new technologies that would improve communication. I had been working six years for an insurance company before I started my advertising agency specialized in digital media. A friend of mine became my business partner. After the two of us created a thorough business plan, we started that new adventure. I put my house as a collateral on a business loan, we started to hire people and launched a huge advertising campaign seeking our first customers.

My partner was responsible for business development. I was handling creative and production. We quickly closed a few deals that allowed us to hire consultants. Those consultants became employees. The business was launched. In two years, we booked close to $1 million of business. We started feeling the winds of success and thought it was just the beginning of a great adventure.

After two years, sales started to slow down and I wondered why. We now had a team of four sales people including my partner. Something was happening but it could have been just a little hurdle along the way. Just a little bump.

Unfortunately, it was more than that. James, my business partner, was getting sick, going through serious mental and physical problems and did not realize it. He did not realize it until it was too late for him and for us as a business. Unbeknownst to him, he was damaging our relationship with clients and clients started to leave us. I realized that when he was losing tremendous amounts of weight. I then knew something serious was going on.

I had to put an end to the business relationship with him, not only to protect him as he was going downhill putting his health in jeopardy but also for the business. One thing was resolved but another one was popping out slowly but surely: the downfall of the economy. We had signed a big production contract with a Fortune 100 Corporation and that big corporation called us in September of 2008 announcing that they had to cancel the project. The reason that was communicated to me is that budgets had been cut. Why budgets were cut was the big mystery. The problem is that I had already invested in materials and in human resources. Now what was I going to do? That big corporation did not want to pay me for all of this. We had done some pre-production work. Was all of this going to have to be on us? Was that really the way it was supposed to be? A billion dollar corporation against a small advertising agency trying to make it every month through hard work to meet its payroll requirements and to stay afloat? I could not accept that.

So I fought. I gathered signed contracts. I collected all the communication that had happened between us proving that a lot of work had been done and that some investments had to take place in order to meet set deadlines. I had kept all my e-mails, all faxes, all our creative and organized all of this in a folder. The next thing I needed was a good lawyer. The first few lawyers I talked to let me know that there was no chance I could fight and win such a monster. "This company has herds of lawyers, Catherine" they said "and they have the money to support those lawyers. You have no chance of winning this one".

Well, I disagreed. I kept looking for the right assistance and finally found a law firm that was willing to look at my case. The head attorney told me that there was a possibility that I could get some money back but there was no guarantee. I had to be willing to take the risk to lose the money I had to invest to pay him. I decided to proceed. I communicated all the information I had gathered and shared it with my attorney. We communicated back and forth with the firm's attorneys but were going nowhere.

I had to come to the realization that what was being done did not work. The other side was just playing us, trying to postpone the process. They never responded on time. They came up with new allegations. They were being unfair and unethical. They knew that they were dealing with a small fish. I was unsatisfied with the efforts provided by my attorney. I did not see in him the energy and the belief I needed to see. I knew that it would take extraordinary amounts of efforts and extreme faith to win this one and he did not show that. See, the problem is that it is very unusual to find extraordinary people that are ready and willing to fight for the right causes. Most of them just do their jobs. Most of them are following the flow of what they are used to doing. They make a great living by doing the minimum but when it's time to provide beyond normal efforts, they disappear and fade away.

I decided to end that relationship. I was going to go after that big company on my own. I collected all the documents given to my attorney and I was going to fight like no other. The first thing I did is call the other side's attorneys and set up an appointment with them. I told them that I was aware of what they were trying to do. I also told them that I was not going to give up. They did not know yet that I had kept a lot of communication and that I had proofs to go somewhere.

I trusted that there had to be some justice in this world and that justice had to happen right then.

I spent hours reviewing my files, going through every detail. I organized everything by date. I had proofs of all my investments. After a couple of weeks, I knew my case was strong. I was ready. A friend of mine saw what I was doing and asked if I needed help. He was an avid negotiator, extremely savvy with business matters and was appalled by what was happening.

"Catherine, I'm going to help you" he said. "Let's set up a meeting with those guys and let's go for it. Your case is strong. You have all the necessary documents to fight. We can win".

The meeting was set within a couple of hours. We had to do it over the phone as we were dealing with a few attorneys located at different places. Prior to the meeting, I sent them a copy of my files so that they would have a chance to review the details. We were ready.

It took us two hours to go through everything. My friend took over at one point, mentioning past experiences he had, his knowledge of the potential economic problems that were heading our way and the principles of the case that he knew would be considered by a judge. He finished by saying that they had to realize that they could not win.

"You now have two options" he said. "We will lower our prices by 15% if you agree to settle amicably and pay what you owe us right now. If you don't agree to these terms, we will take you to court and will ask for the full amount with interest. You tell us."

A short silence followed. You could feel the tension in the air and hear flies fly and hearts beat. And then: "You will receive a check within 2 weeks. The case is closed".

They hung up.

My friend and I looked at each other with awe. We had won. We won a case that other attorneys said we could not win. And we did it ourselves.

That day I learnt one thing. I learnt that you and only you has the passion to fight for your rights. The power of your beliefs can take you far, much farther than you can often imagine. If you believe that something isn't right and that you want to see justice happen because you know what is right, you need to fight. You need to fight not only for yourself but for others to show that being ethical is critical and that unlawful attitude is not accepted. I was not going to give up to intimidation. My belief and my attitude was felt by the other party. They knew I was going to fight until I could not fight anymore and they were not willing to go that route as they also knew that I could win because of all the evidence I had carefully kept.

Never stop believing that justice exists. Yes you will face sharks and tigers and horrible monsters that have no principle or ethics but if you know that you are doing the right thing, you need to proceed and go for it. And you will win. It is this "never giving up" attitude that will take you far.

This was the beginning of the company's downfall. There was a reason why that big corporation had cancelled that contract. They knew that the business landscape was changing. They knew that a major recession was hitting the country and the world. And they were right. Although I was exhilarated by the success of getting paid by them, I quickly saw things getting worse and worse. It was getting very hard to close deals. Regular customers started to not order as much. Payments were delayed. Accounts receivable suffered and cash flow became a huge problem. We quickly started to not be able to meet our obligations. I felt the world was on my shoulders. I became exhausted and scared. Every day, as I arrived at the office, I was wondering how long I was going to be able to do this. How long was I going to have to go through such stress?

As business was not coming in and income was reduced, I had to start using my savings to make payroll. I had to start asking friends and family for help to keep the business going. I did not want to give up.

After a few more months, the trend had not changed and I could not continue losing money that way. I had to make a decision to close the business. I knew that I was going to lose everything I had but I had no choice. I knew that I was putting my house in jeopardy as it had been placed as a collateral. I had debts and obligations I was not going to be able to meet. That was the end of that dream.

I quickly learnt that I was going to be personally liable for all the business debts. I had no way of meeting those obligations. I had to file for bankruptcy. I announced this to my staff who were devastated. But instead of helping, they tried to take things away from me. They took materials, furniture and anything they could put their hands on. I had given everything to them, but got nothing back. No gratitude. Nothing. They knew I had lost everything I had but they were asking for more and even threatened to sue me if I did not pay them to the dime.

A few weeks later, the business was closed, the offices left vacant. I was sitting on the bench close to the porch of my house wondering what had happened. It felt like a huge tornado had gone by and had taken away everything on its passage. I looked up towards the sky asking God for some guidance and wondering why all of this had happened. My head was in cotton, unable to clearly see anymore. I felt lost, scared and had not idea how to get back on track, on the road to a new life. I closed my eyes. Another day was gone.

Now, almost two years later, I know exactly what happened:

1. I took some risks by launching this business. I believed in it and gave it all I had. I planned it all and thought I had it all perfect. I knew there was a chance it would work out well and a chance it would not. I just did it.

2. I hired friends of friends and realized they were not qualified enough for the jobs they were supposed to do. I did not go through the proper hiring process and

did not spend time going through the right interviewing processes. I hired people that ended up being lazy and who took advantage of me. They knew I was trusting and instead of working hard to show gratitude towards that trust, they abused it. If you build a business, please don't make that same mistake. Make the proper selection with a full skill analysis. Take the time to interview and select by qualifications and personality not because they know someone you know. I also paid for this mistake dearly.

3. I did not have enough financial backings to sustain the business long enough in case of potential hardship (economical, health or environmental). Hardship took place. Cash flow was insufficient. And doors closed.

4. I hired accountants that were not at the top of their games. They spent hours working on the bookkeeping trying to "fix" what they claimed the previous accountant did not do right. They did not alert me close to the end that if I did not pay the company payroll taxes, I was going to be liable for them personally, despite the bankruptcy. Still now, I am battling with the IRS that claims that some payroll were not declared and that I should pay them. I thought I was dealing with true professionals when I was not. Once again, I probably should have had two accountants so that they could check each other out.

5. I hired business consultants that only knew how to take money from me but never delivered results that

were tangible enough to make a difference.

6. And lastly, I was managing my business from a micro perspective, not paying enough attention to the macro world, the economical statistics and trends. I should have paid attention to the signs that were given to me coming from various angles. But I decided to ignore them. A business on its own is nothing. A business as part of a well-informed entity aware of its environment, its threats and its opportunities builds all necessary tools to prepare for the future, be it positive or challenging.

I took some risks, trusted the wrong people, made a few mistakes and destroyed my financial strength. But I don't regret anything. Why? Because this has been the most valuable lesson of my life. Should I decide to do it again, I would know exactly what and what not to do. Plus this experience has made me stronger, and has taught me to look at what I am doing from a broader perspective. It is quite fascinating to me as I am now always stepping back when something happens. Like an eagle, I have come to realize that in order to find the right pray (the right solution), I have to fly over it a few times and looked at it from all angles before I know for sure that it is the one that I want to grab and devour. Like the eagle, I analyze the situation with different perspectives and know when to dive and when to abstain. I now know when the clouds are too deep for me to pierce and when the sun is bright and warm enough for me to soar in. And if the results of my decisions are not exactly what I had expected, I look at them with more wisdom and less anger as in the end, whether I cry, I scream or I make myself sick, the reality won't change but for sure I will hurt my heart pressure and my overall health.

Not worth it!

TAKE THE GOOD MOMENTS LIFE BRINGS YOU. TAKE THEM WITHOUT RESERVATIONS, AS YOU DON'T KNOW HOW LONG THEY WILL LAST. LEARN TO BE ALONE AND TO ENJOY YOUR OWN COMPANY. THEN, YOU WILL BE ABLE TO FULLY ENJOY THE COMPANY OF OTHERS. A DOOR THAT CLOSES MEANS ANOTHER ONE WILL OPEN SOON. TAKE RISKS. LIVE YOUR DREAMS. GET THE RIGHT ADVICE BUT ALWAYS LISTEN TO THE STILL VOICE WITHIN YOU TO GUIDE YOUR DECISIONS. AND REMEMBER IN THE END, NO ONES CARES FOR YOU AS MUCH AS YOU DO. IF YOU WANT AN EXTRAORDINARY LIFE, HAVE THE GUTS TO BE AN EXTRAORDINARY YOU, AND ONLY DEPEND ON YOU TO MAKE IT HAPPEN!

Success is getting what you want. Happiness is wanting what you get.
- Dale Carnegie

REALITY #10
WHEN PAIN HITS, HIT THE ROAD OF YOUR SOUL

Do you know that worrying is completely sterile? You can worry for hours, I can guarantee you that it will not change the outcome of your life. Or at least, it won't make that outcome better. It can only make it worse. So many of us even worry about the fact that we worry. Is that screwed up or what??? We will not prevent bad things from happening because we worry more. Worrying actually impacts our body in surprising ways. When excessive, worrying can lead to feelings of high anxiety and make us become physically ill. I know. I got a stomach ulcer from it! So what should you do to stop worrying?

First, recognize that you are worrying. Become completely aware of it. Pick up a piece a paper and write down "I am worrying. I am right now recognizing that I am worrying. I need to stop worrying. It will hurt me".

Second, write down all the negative thoughts that are

going through your mind. When you are done, read them one more time, take that piece of paper and burn it. Make sure you don't set your house on fire by doing so. I don't want to be responsible for major sudden house fires all over the country!]

One of the most challenging times in my life was when I knew I was going to leave my second husband, Larry. I had lived with him two years in Hong-Kong when my daughter was a young baby. We then moved to the U.S., going back to his country. This is when everything changed. Our life in Hong-Kong had been unreal. All was paid by his company. I had a full time maid. Life was good. But then reality hit. I had to build a new life in the U.S. I had to find a job right away, we lived with his parents for a few months and we had to move several times, as jobs changed. After four moves, we finally ended up in San Diego where my husband found a new job. I absolutely loved it there. We had a nice home, I had a part-time job and was studying graphic and web design the rest of the time. I felt happy, at last and could see myself staying there forever.

But things don't happen like that do they? My husband lost his job and had to look for a new one. After a few weeks, he found one in Reno, NV where we had to move. We sold our house and there we were again, traveling towards a new destination, facing the unknown. I was scared that time, although I had done this several times but for some reason, I knew that this time was going to lead to more unplanned changes.

We arrived in Reno, rented a house and attempted to build a new life. But stress quickly took over. Larry had a hard time dealing with my daughter's tantrums and starting to demonstrate violent behaviors. Sadness, resentment and anger were my daily friends and soon I had no idea how I was going to continue going through life in these conditions. Here is an exert of what I wrote then:

"I feel like I am being poured out like a drink offering and the time has come for my departure. I have fought the good fight, I have finished the race, I have kept the faith. My body itches all over. I have no hunger, I want to vomit all the time. My body and mind are tired but I cannot stop. I need to tire myself out physically to be able to cope with the events, to calm down.

"I feel betrayed and want to get rid of the betrayer, of the one who has been hurting and disrespecting me for so long. I am not sure how to do it yet. I am not sure if I will be able to face everything on my own. I have anger in me and this anger is pushing me to react, to be myself without letting him influence me anymore. I want to be me, just me. I have buried the real me during all these years to conform to his lifestyle, to his ideas, to his extremism. I felt I had no choice, having no financial strength and a child to support in a foreign country. I wanted to believe I would be OK and this was the price to pay to survive and move on to a better life.

"During the last 2 years, I have cried when hurt by his selfish behavior. Very often, I wanted to leave him, to free myself from this heavy load that was suffocating me. (Interestingly enough, this is when I started to have strong asthma attacks.)

"Thanks to a good job that I now have in Reno, I feel financially stronger, stronger than Larry who keeps loosing his jobs one after the other. Finally, I feel I have my word to say. I want to explode, express my feelings, the feelings I kept for myself for so long. I am tired of having his ex-wife over my head, the reason of all his rejections and life-stopping effects. She has always been the reason for not doing anything.

"He always described me as an angel, because I was always positively acknowledging everything he said, following each of his gestures, helping and devoting myself to him all the way. I wanted to believe in him so much that I treated him as a God. He had no barrier with me, no obstacle, an always agreeable woman. He had me under his power.

"Although a few times I saw him act violently with Adelle, I swallowed my anger and had to follow his attitude, by fear of him getting angry at me. As soon as I showed the slightest disagreement with the way he was treating Adelle, he looked at me with killer eyes, so mad it scared me to death.

"My anger grew stronger and stronger but I still wanted to believe that he had so many other qualities that these angers were inconsequent. And for so long, I said nothing, nothing because if I dared say anything, he would look at me with these eyes full of anger, making me feel lower than dirt. I am developing feelings of strong hatred. Interestingly enough, I still have some compassion for him at the thought of him having no more job and potentially no more wife. So, sometimes I show myself loving and willing to help. Of course, he accepts it, feeling lost himself. But then, his behavior shifts and his coldness and irritation, emotional violence, comes back like a wild cat jumping at my face. So I react and protect myself.

"The difference now is that I have to talk. I cannot just swallow everything like I have for so long. I cannot keep my disagreements for myself. Now I know that I can be on my own, although I am aware this will be hard for both Adelle and I. So I talk, and talk, and talk again and Larry does not like it of course. Adelle is the only barrier to creating my freedom from him. It is because of her that I am still trying to find ways to improve the situation between the two of us.

"Deep inside me, this is over. I don't have any respect for him anymore. I cannot touch him anymore. I never felt I had a protection that a husband gives to his wife. I always felt I was on my own. I always had to work, sometimes in hard conditions, I always said to him that I did not feel like I had a man, a protector in my life. I feel like

I have been carrying the burden all the way, all by myself.

"I want to be freed from this burden. I want an open blue sky with a good potential future. I want to feel young and beautiful again. Larry makes me feel old and unattractive. I want to feel loved. I want to laugh and conquer the world. I want to live with no black clouds over my head. It is now time for the thunder to burn the scarves, time for the rain to clean the dirt, time for the clouds to be pushed away by the wind. Time for a clear blue sky..."

Understand that whatever you are going through, there is this strength inside of you, ready to arise. It is waiting for your signal to start growing and guide you towards incredible accomplishments and deep well-being. Accept to be alone. Face yourself. It is scary to face oneself. Many people cannot stay by themselves and admit it. My ex husband has always been telling me: "Catherine, you know I cannot stay alone". Facing oneself is one of the most difficult exercise in the process of individual growth. It is also the only way to reach peace and balance. It is the only way to understand our purpose, to surround ourselves with the right people and to develop true, deep happiness. Anything else is only surreal. Anything else is superficial.

How many people are jumping from one relationship to another? How many people cannot accept the slow recovery of a dramatic event like a divorce, a death of any dramatic change that can occur in life? Recovery is a very slow process. You need to give it time as if you don't, you will pay for it, one way or the other.

My ex-husband, Larry, went on the Internet one month after our divorce to find a new partner. He made a search, selected 3 candidates who most corresponded to his requirements and made one final selection. Two months after our divorce, he was dating this new woman and claimed loud and clear that he was in love. Three months after our divorce, I asked him to come back for us all as the situation was extremely painful for both my daughter and I. He claimed again that he was in love and that he could not do this to his new "love". He said this would not be fair to her. I told him he was dreaming and that the "love" he thought he felt was only infatuation. And, infatuation is the most superficial feeling one can have. It never lasts long. With no deep love of oneself inside, infatuation dies into total emptiness very quickly. And yet, it had all started like a dream:

"Hello, this is Larry Brandborn. Can I help you?"

"Hello Larry. This is Catherine. We met in Taiwan a couple of weeks ago. Do you remember me?"

"Catherine?" he replied "Of course, how are you. It is so nice to hear from you!"

"Well, I was thinking about you. I was wondering if you have any plans of coming to Taiwan again, and I was also thinking of visiting Hong-

Kong. After all, I am not in Asia every day and thought it may be my chance to visit that great city."

"Catherine" he quickly added, "If you come to Hong-Kong, you have to come visit me. I'd love to show you around".

"OK" I added with excitement. "When would be a good time for you?"

"Anytime next week would be great. Do you think you can make it?

"I am sure I can. Let me check the flights. I will call you back to confirm". I hung up. "Mom" I screamed with excitement. "He invited over to visit Hong-Kong. What do you think? Should I go? Is that too much?"

"Too much of what?" she answered. "Too much of joy, too much of discovery, too much fun?. What are you talking about? Go, go, don't wait one more minute. Reserve your flight and go".

Five days later, I landed in Hong-Kong. The airport was located downtown and you literally felt like you were landing on top of the buildings. It was a scary sight. One of my numerous cousins happened to live in Hong-Kong that year. He invited me to stay over with him and his family, so I did. Larry was waiting for me at the airport. I was anxiously walking toward the exit when I recognized his face in the middle of the crowd.

He was waving at me and hugged me when he saw me.

"So good to see you again" he whispered in my ears.

"Nice to see you too, Larry" I answered back.

"Let me drive you to your cousin's place. You can spend the night there and I will pick you up tomorrow morning for a city tour. Is that OK?"

"It is perfect" I replied with excitement.

I had not seen my cousin for five years and there he was with his wife that I had never met and his nine-month old little boy. What a thrill! I was with some of my family members in Hong-Kong and I was going to spend the day with a hot guy the next day. What a life!

My cousin lived in a four-bedroom apartment in a nice complex in the suburb of Hong-Kong. Rentals are extremely expensive in Hong-Kong, which forces most people to live in the City surroundings. It is not unusual to pay $10,000/month for a flat downtown so most people can't afford it unless it is paid by their company. He worked for a large French Corporation as an International Business Development Representative. He was doing quite well. His wife was from the Philippines. He had met her during a business trip to Manila. She was fun, uplifting and full of energy. They were good to me and it was great for me to be around such great energy.

The next day, Larry came to pick me up. He gave me a tour of Hong-Kong. I discovered how busy this central international platform was. Outside markets fill the streets living hardly any space for people to walk forcing anyone to literally push their way through the crowd. You could find anything from pirated software to live chicken. Even snakes were kept in cages for people to purchase. There was this unique smell running through the streets. A mix of cooked food, live stock and people's sweat. It was in average 95 degrees with 90% humidity. I was constantly sweating and of course, my hair that I carefully straightened that morning had become frizzy and wild giving me that just awoken look that I could not stand.

After a day of touring, Larry took me to his apartment. The apartment was in the Hyatt building in the Wanchai area of Hong-Kong. Wanchai is the business center of Hong-Kong where most exhibitions take place. At the 12th floor of that building was a beautiful garden with tennis courts and swimming pools, with a big play area for children. The garden dominated the Hong-Kong busy harbor and gave sight to the other side, Kowloon. It was fascinating to me to discover such luxury in the middle of this crowded busy city that seemed to fight pollution while developing pieces of heaven in its center. Larry's flat was on the 21st floor. He shared it with a student. After a great dinner in a typical Chinese restaurant, Larry took my back to my cousin's place to spend the night. The next day, we had to say good-bye. I was happy I had a chance to discover Hong-Kong, see my cousin and get to know Larry a little better. I was still not sure about how he viewed my pregnancy. However, the world was open and anything possible.

He came a few weeks later to visit me in Taipei where we exchanged our first kiss. He then visited me in France several times and shared the wonderful times of my pregnancy's evolution. We fell in love and made plans to live together. It would be Hong-Kong as Larry had to stay there a few more years. I would sell all I had, leave my place and move to Asia.

It's July 14th and I am lying down in bed, exhausted. My mother is sitting next to me. That day, our country is celebrating its National Day and Fireworks pop everywhere. I am tired. I fall asleep. Midnight comes and so do my waters. I wake up suddenly feeling this incredible warm wave of liquid. My baby is coming.

"Mom" I scream. "I think the baby is coming. It is time. Please take me to the hospital!"

"Oh my god" my mother answers with great anxiety. She then calls Joe her husband who immediately gets the car ready. "Get your bag, get the baby's bag. Let's go"

A few minutes later, we are in the car driving towards the Grenoble hospital where I am supposed to deliver.

Joe, scared of having to deliver a baby in his car, was burning all red lights.

I delivered my baby after twenty hours of painful labor. Her birth dad was not there, nor was Larry. He had no time to make it on time. But all my aunts and cousins and uncles were present to cheer and welcome this new life that was going to change mine forever.

A month later, I sold all my belongings and found myself at the Charles de Gaulles airport with my baby and two suitcases ready to get on the plane to Hong-Kong. I had decided to take the risk of leaving everything and starting a new life with Larry.

Larry and I had a few wonderful years. We lived in Hong-Kong where we had a full time maid. Adelle was a baby and that help was very much appreciated since I was working full time. Working full-time in Hong-Kong means working Monday thru Saturday included. Sunday was the only day off. Larry was traveling all over Asia and I spent most of the time alone with Adelle and our maid. It was almost impossible to have a deep and true relationship with him (now that I think about it) as as soon as we started to get to know each other, he was on his way out. Our life in Hong-Kong was therefore quite superficial. There, I learnt how to fit in the crowd as everywhere we went, it was crowded. I also learnt to make my way by pushing others, typical Hong-Kong tradition. After a while, I started to get used to the busy outside and to the smell of live fish in the street. I was scrolling the streets with Adelle on my back, walking up and down the stairs and miles of walkways.

Circumstances took us back to the U.S. sooner than planned. This is when the downfall was initiated and the sorrow and hurt launched. Pain hit and forced me to look at new avenues to escape, to survive and to live as best as I could. It forced me to grow like I had never grown before.

So my dear friend, remember that when you feel pain, do all that you can to look inside of yourself. Work at understanding why you are going through what you are going through. All that happens in our lives happens for a reason. I first had a hard time believing in this concept as it is quite a harsh one to admit when you are in the middle of the storm. The best thing to do when you feel lost, scared and uncertain about everything is to calm down and know that this too shall pass.

There is always a beautiful sun after a big storm. We just need to show enough patience and enough understanding to let the storm go by and learn about each and everyone one of its thunders trike. You will go on. Life will go on and if you don't give up to the heavy loads of pain, you will get out of this journey stronger, happier and more balanced.

ACCORDING TO ANCIENT INDIAN SCRIPTURE PATANJALI, THE IGNORANCE OR FALSE KNOWL-EDGE WHICH IS THE MOTHER OF ALL OTHER PAIN CAN BE AVOIDED OR CONTROLLED THROUGH MEDITATION. ONE SHOULD MEDITATE UPON ONE'S TRUE SELF, SOUL OR ATMAN ONLY, BECAUSE IT IS THE REAL AND ETERNAL THING ONE POSSESSES. FOR MEDITATION, ONE SHOULD SIT DOWN IN A LOTUS POSTURE WITH EYES CLOSED. THEN ONE SHOULD CONCENTRATE ONE'S MIND ON TRIKUTI WHICH IS A POINT IN BETWEEN THE EYEBROWS AND ABOVE THE NOSE. REGULAR PRACTICE IN THE MORNING AND EVENING AT LEAST FOR HALF AN HOUR TAKES ONE'S MIND CLOSER TO TRUE SELF.

Adopt the pace of nature: her secret is patience.
- Ralph Waldo Emerson

REALITY #11
HORMONAL CHALLENGES

And came the hormones! I can't tell you how many times I have heard women say that something happens when you turn fourty. Of course, I never believe it! "Nothing is going to happen to me" I explained. "I am on top of that". Well, I quickly discovered that I was not at all on top of that. Hormones create mood swings and total lack of desire. Hormones made me become another person, a total stranger that I could not relate to. In fact, I hated that other person. I became more of a loner, in need of calm times and meditation, pushing away all that was getting close. I would wake up one day hating the whole world not wanting to live anymore. And I never understood why.

The hard thing is not being able to explain what is happening to you. You face a man that you love and you tell him that you really don't want to spend time with him. You tell him that you don't want to live anymore, that you are just too tired to do anything and that you are probably not the right woman for him. How is he supposed to react? Not well, I guarantee you that one!

So one day, during those moods, I came to my then fiancé

and told him that I could not do that. I could not marry him as I felt I was not a "good enough" partner. My moods had convinced me that I would never be able to make him happy as I was not happy and balanced myself. So I gave him the ring back! I placed the ring on his desk and told him that this was not working for me. I could not become his wife as I felt I could not fulfill that task well enough. I can't tell you how often I regretted that gesture but felt that I had no choice. I felt powerless, forced to retire from this unhealthy spiral I found myself in.

The worse thing about those states that I call "hormonal earthquakes" is that there is no logical explanation to it. I am a business woman right? So, I always try to find logical explanations to facts so that I can apply a fix to them and move on with the right solutions. Well, I was not able to do this with my states. I just could not explain them. The only way for me to handle those was to decide that I was no good and that the relationship could not flourish healthily because I was so unstable. And of course, this is what he understood and believed. After all, this is what I kept telling him. Why would he believe any different? He said that to me many times: "I believe what people tell me. Why would I not?"

James and I lived six months together after I gave him the ring back. Then, he decided to leave and have his own place as this was not working out for him. I kept rejecting him, telling him that I could not make him happy and that I was probably not the right woman for him. Now, I wish I had found the miracle remedy to prevent me from saying those words. How can I push away a man so easily? How could I do this? Now I know. The only way that I could have done that is that it was not truly me.

The woman that had given him the ring back was not truly me. In those times, I became some kind of an alien, a dark side that was taking over my soul, my spirit and my body. That dark side came out so many times that James started to believe that it was the true me, but it was not. Then he started disliking that person he had in front of him because that person was just creating hurt, damaging his life, his health, his balance and his drive for happiness. I was hurting the person that was most important in my life without being able to control it.

We lived apart but we still shared some wonderful moments of joy, happiness and intimacy. Those moments happened when I felt free, when I felt myself and when I was out of the hormonal alienation. The worse is that those moments were often followed by moments of rejection when I fell back into my unexplained moods. James of course did not understand. "How can you be so close and intimate with me one day and reject me the next?". Of course, who would have understood that? I did not understand that either and each time it happened, I retired into my shell trying to hide, ashamed, hurt and unable to decide what to do next.

This lasted a few months. James kept saying that he was

OK in our relationship when in fact he was not. And one day, James decided to call it quit. Again, I needed to be alone to face my own discomfort, my own fears and my own inabilities to deal with myself.

I could not even react when he said that he had had enough. "I can't be a part-time lover" he said. "I want a healthy relationship. I want a wife. I want a happy life with the woman I love and you can't offer this". I listened and turned my back as again, I did not understand. I turned my back, went home, numb and unable to react. "I am sorry" I said. "I am not stable. I know".

Hormonal inbalance is something you need to take seriously. The first step is to recognize that this is what you are going through. You wake up sad and exhausted for not reason. You are depressed and can't explain it. You hate the world when the world has done nothing to you. You don't recognize yourself as you become a monster wanting to destroy everything... Often, these are signs of a lack of something in your body that you need to watch and examin.

It is hard to determine what it is you are lacking. I have consulted many doctors and none of them have given me the magical remedy that put everything back into order.

Every month, the female hormones estrogen and progesterone are produced. When estrogen and progesterone levels do not balance, it will cause a dramatic effect on your body and your overall health. The hormonal inbalance can affect your ovaries, your fallopian tubes and your uterus. You may feel certains pains you never did before. For me, the most challenging factor has been the mood swings and the unexplained fatigue I felt at certain times of the month.

Here are the typical signs and symptoms of hormonal inbalance:

- Changes in menstruation
- Acne
- Basal body temperature
- Oily skin
- Excessive hair growth
- Fatigue
- Dizziness
- Allergy symptoms
- Anxiety
- Low sex drive
- Headaches
- Weight gain
- Depression
- Endometriosis
- Water retention
- Premenstrual Syndrome (PMS)
- Urinary tract infections (UTI's)

I, of course, recommend that you see a specialist as soon as you feel those symptoms on a regular basis. I am not a doctor and will not tell you what to do.

What I can tell you is that I have tried several things and what has worked for me is what a homeopath told me to do. He literally changed my life when he explained to me that the body has a tendency to create additional hormones when there is a lack of nutrients.

This lack of nutrients forces the body to generate substances trying to rebalance the whole system. He therefore told me to do everything I could to make sure that my body had all the necessary nutrients to avoid its natural reaction of trying to balance out itself. Here is what I have been doing everyday for the last year, which has changed my life for the better:

- When I get up, I drink a big glass of water. I take two teaspoon of liquid chlorophyll which is a natural disinfectant and 1 teaspoon of molasses which provides the calcium my body needs.- I drink 2 table spoon of liquid multi-vitamins.- I take some vitamin B 100 and I have a good breakfast about half an hour after I wake up. (you may have some multivitamins in capsules or pills but the liquid ones are the most efficient ones - remember that our body is mostly made of water and will absorb liquid better then pills)

- I drink lots of fluids all day long. It is essential to stay hydrated.

- I eat a light healthy meal at lunch and drink green tea the rest of the afternoon

- I eat a fruit or two in the afternoon

- I eat a healthy meal in the evening and end up the day with a herbal tea with drops of Wild Yam and sarsaparilla that helps sustain phytoestrogen levels.

- I apply bio-identical progesterone cream on my body every day.

Again I am not a doctor and can't tell you that this will work for you. What I can tell you is this diet has made a difference in my moods, my energy levels and my general health. I feel the difference if I don't do it.

Remember one thing: you know yourself and your body better than anyone else out there. Try things and adjust to your needs. I truly believe that there is no one single remedy that fits all. You have to try and adjust until you find what works for you.

Hormonal imbalance can start early, in your thirties and even younger. Typically, estrogen levels start to decline at the time of perimenopause, which is prior to the actual onset of menopause. Estrogen levels also fall after a woman has given birth or when she is breast feeding.

My goal is to create awareness about how you can be impacted by hormonal imbalance and to help recognize that the symptoms you may experience are caused by a lack of one or more specific hormones.

Do you research, talk to various types of doctors including naturopaths and homeopaths.

You will be surprised as to what you will learn. Just be open-minded and curious and you will find the right guidance.

MORE THAN FOURTY MILLION POSTMENOPAUSAL WOMEN IN THE U.S. CAN EXPECT TO LIVE A THIRD OF THEIR LIVES AFTER MENOPAUSE. IF YOU APPROACH MENOPAUSE FROM A HOLISTIC STANDPOINT, IT SHIFTS FROM A HORMONAL DEFICIENCY TO A HORMONAL SHIFT. THIS IS PART OF THE AGING PROCESS AND THE MORE WE EMBRACE IT, THE BETTER WE WILL LIVE IT. CELEBRATE AND RESPECT YOUR MENOPAUSE. LISTEN TO YOUR BODY AND PAY ATTENTION TO SIGNS. LOOK AT THIS PROCESS WITH A POSITIVE ATTITUDE, STAY INFORMED AND MAKE CHOICES THAT FIT YOU.

A people that values its privileges above its principles soon loses both.
- Dwight D. Eisenhower

REALITY #12
CULTURAL DEGRADATION AND TV NON SENSE

To all of you women of heart, brains and sensitivity, I am really worried about what is happening in our culture and I am now saying out loud that it is time to do something about it.

Let's start with what the TV networks are putting on our screens. Nonsense, degradation, stupidity and vulgarity. I am appalled by which levels we went down. I am talking of course about the reality shows that are filling out the network schedules as quickly as the plague spread over our world in the 1700s. This is serious people.

Here are a few samples of what our children are exposed daily and of what indirectly influences their behavior, their beliefs and their values:

1. Real Housewives of New York City, of Beverly Hills, of the moon (coming up soon)
2. Kate + 8
3. Jersey Shore, Jerseylicious
4. Bad Girls Club
5. The Kardashian

Now let me tell you what these shows do to us: they degrade women by pointing out their superficial behavior. They portray women as sex objects showing off more and more their body and less and less of their brains. Are we nuts to encourage those shows by watching them? Haven't we fought enough for liberation, respect and equality with men? Do you think this is doing us a favor?

Take the example of Real Housewives. We are watching spoiled brats with more money than they know what to do with telling us about their purposeless lives and their limited thinking. Those women have gone through some many plastic surgeries that they look like old dolls that the dog chewed on too many times. To you women on these shows, why do you do that? Is you life that boring? Don't you have anything better to do? Do you realize what you are doing? And aren't you ashamed of showing off all your wealth and the thousand pairs of shoes you have when most people are struggling to just feed their children and keep a roof on top of their heads? What is wrong with you? And what is wrong with you TV networks? Where are your morals? Where are your values? Is it all about money? Where are you taking our society? Don't you think you have huge responsibility in our children emotional growth and in our cultural well-being? Are you only aware of the damage you are doing?

Now have a look at Jersey Shore. We now have low life people (Snooky, and all others on the show) being portrayed and treated as stars! Ah! We bring them on TV shows across the country and have them talk. The sad thing is that they have nothing to say that is worth listening to. They have no class, no education and no self-control. Sickening.

I am begging all of you women that still have some common sense and sanity to start a full boycott of those shows by first not watching them and preventing your children to watch them and second by writing letters to the networks —the first ones being BRAVO and OXYGEN— two networks claiming to offer programs women have demanded to see letting them know that they have to stop featuring such degradation on our TV screens.

All of this scares me as it represents a cultural tendency that can quickly shift to trends that will be hard to deviate and change. We are heading towards a modern type of Roman Empire: a total decadence of human beings and particularly of women. The Roman Empire was the time when arose the race of unlovely unattractive and even often totally repulsive women for their attainments as intriguers, poisoners, adulteress and even destroyers of the Roman home, who taught every one with whom they came into contact with to live for themselves alone and be completely selfish. Hmmm, does this sound familiar?

When Christianity saw the effects on civilization of this unbridled liberty among women, it inevitably and rightly reacted towards a more stringent less liberal than the Roman view. The Roman emancipation of women had to be annulled when women were no longer able to enjoy their freedom aright. And so the new tendency was in the direction of the Greek ideal whereby the woman was the humble servant of her husband and no more.

In the light of this analysis, I hope that you all realize what is going on in our culture and that if nothing is done to stop that trend, our family balance will be destroyed, women will become either total dictators or total slaves, men will have no clue where to stand and our children will be left to themselves to lead their lives. I now joke about the possible disappearance of true men and created a new name for untrue men. A NAM (my creation) or a *Non Accomplished Male*, is the growing creation of our sick society. A NAM is unable to take men's responsibilities, depends on his wife/girlfriend to earn a living and has no idea or envy to take care of children, the house pets or the house. A NAM is the type of men starring in shows like Jersey Shores and others even worse.

So imagine that. Not only do we have a growing number of NAMs, we are now encouraging sexual exhibitionism of women with the same total lack of responsibilities of healthy motherhood as role model for their children. Where are our children heading to? Can anyone doubt that in such state of sexual overstimulation there will naturally develop a withdrawal of interest from sex itself? What I fear will happen is that this obscenity displayed and now seemingly accepted everywhere will quickly take away desire and therefore cancel out any chance of having healthy relationships and marriages. And if we end with a majority of NAMs, that may resolve our over-population issue for good!

Is that what we women want? Do we want our real men

to turn away in disgust from such growing shamelessness? Do we want our real men to lose respect for pure and healthy womanhood? Unbridled liberty of action and of talk (the most frequent word in those shows is the word f~ or f~ing) may very well lead to extinction of the little respect that remains in our culture for women.

Does this make you think at all? Do you still want to watch these shows or do you want to do something about it?

The movements that are taking place are the demonstration of a deep societal crisis. Why are those shows so popular? Because people in America have stopped dreaming for themselves. They live through "stars" like Snooky to create excitement in their lives. They have given up on their own dreams and desires. They have become lazy. They bow to low-level individuals that most of the time have no education, no upbringing and no principles.

This may sound harsh but in harsh times rise harsh realities. We need to seriously ask ourselves why we fell to such lows. Why are we allowing ourselves to lose our values?

There is so much we women can do. The world needs us. We complement men and bring qualities they don't in many life settings. Come on! There's a reason why God created a man and a woman, don't you think? I know that I have been mad at men for a long time but I also know that I need them to be here. I know a lot of women out there are irritated by what is happening but I also know that a lot of you strive for something greater.

Let's not fall into such decadence. Let's continue being wholesome and educate ourselves to play a bigger role in the society.

It is this growing feeling of frustration that pushed me to study again in my mid twenties. I wanted to learn more and become smarter and stronger. I had to go back to school. I had to build a bigger purpose to my life. I then decided to enroll in a college to work towards an MBA in marketing/management. I faced a lot of counter forces after this decision was made. "You will never make it. This is much too challenging for you!" or "How can you start studying again that much when you have a full time job?".

Remember, in France, it is unusual to start studying after you start a career. It is not like here in the U.S. where you can start a new career anytime, go back to college and learn to become somebody new. These comments came from one ear and left right from the other. I did not care anymore of what other people were saying. I had a goal that I knew was right. There was no other alternative. I had to do it.

So, a few weeks later, I took a few tests and was admitted into the College in Grenoble France. Not only did I manage to keep my job with reduced hours but I also got a student financial help from the French government. I spent four years exclusively working and studying. At that time, I had moved with my father who was living alone with our three horses and two dogs. I was getting up every morning at 5 a.m. to take care of the horses, then prepare breakfast and get ready to go to work. At 8 a.m., I was at work and left my office at 4 p.m. to go to school. From 4 p.m. to 8 p.m., I was at school studying. It took me a half hour to get home every night.

Once home, I prepared dinner and I and started studying from 9 p.m. to midnight to finally go to bed. I did this for 4 years. It became my routine and I had found a natural rhythm. During that time of non-stop work, I did not question what I was doing. I knew it was right. I knew it was my only alternative to accomplish my dreams.

To the comments I had 4 years later that I would never make it, I responded that I not only made it but I ended up first of my class and first of the whole school division with a grade of 18 out of 20. I had set in my mind that I was going to become the best and my actions and thoughts were programmed to reach that goal. The body and the mind have an incredible potential.

This degree opened the door to a job of International Sales Director in a local foundry that was manufacturing cast iron parts. They were having some trouble with the national market and needed someone to help them develop their sales abroad. I was a great candidate being also fluent in 3 foreign languages, which is greatly needed when you want to travel and negotiate in foreign countries. My job was to market and sell cast iron parts all over the world. Travel was a must. I spent 80% of my time traveling. I chose destinations that very few people would have chosen. I hired agents in Algeria, Bahrein, Dubai, Germany, Sweden, England, Spain. I walked the streets of Bahrein surrounded by security guards as women were not always welcomed.

I traveled to Algeria in times of war, when Algerians fought among themselves, killed themselves and targeted French citizens. I was there walking the streets of Algiers with no fear, believing in my mission so strongly that no one was able to change my route. I was determined to do my job and knew what I was doing was right. I managed to get an agent, negotiated with top executives of some of the largest national companies and brought back purchasing orders to my company that no one would have ever dreamt of – and these orders came from countries where women are most unpopular and disrespected.

My boss could not believe his eyes. He had been trying to get deals with these countries for many years, unsuccessfully. Nothing is impossible as long as we understand that the only barriers we face are the barriers we set for ourselves.

I opened doors of companies in Algeria that were managed by people who had been in war with my country and that were ready to die for their rights. I encountered women journalists there that were living with cyanide pills in their pockets, by fear of being caught by some Algerian extremist groups. "We have to do this" they said "Otherwise we know we would be going through terrible torture and suffering. If we are caught, we will swallow this pill to avoid unsustainable pain".

I met hundreds of people, discovered new lands and new countries. I shifted my focus of divorce to a focus of work and travel. I brought back hundreds of new orders that enabled the company to survive and focus their energy in a different way. My determination to succeed grew by the day. I became very determined to create a positive impact somewhere, somehow. I needed positive in my life. I wanted to become unique, wanted and successful, and so I did. I proved wrong to many people who told me that what I wanted to do was impossible as no reasonable individual would do it.

I developed a thirst for knowledge and power. My world traveling taught me how to deal with many different cultures. I was fascinated by the diversity of cultures and thinking processes people of this earth could have. We might have a small world, but what a diversity there is! One factor that can be viewed as terribly painful in one country can be seen as some wonderful event in another. One way to dress in one country is not acceptable in another. Death in Asia is considered the beginning of life. People sing and dance during funerals. They wear white. It is a demonstration of love: a new beginning.

One way to behave and talk in one country is totally impolite and inconsiderate in another. How many times have I seen Chinese people spit in the street, at the pool or in a restaurant with no problem and looked at it in a totally disgusted way? For them, it is OK to spit anywhere they want. For them, it is not OK to use a tissue to blow your nose.

I decided to work at conditioning my body by both exercising my mind to think positively and exercise my body to be stronger. These exercises included meditation, yoga, and any kind of physical activity. I created quiet moments during which I put my mind at rest. I went for regular walks and sat down somewhere where the only sounds I could hear were the ones of nature. I closed my eyes, breathed deeply and meditated. I relaxed my mind and created emptiness around me. I let my thoughts wander and tried to dissociate my mind from my body to start a new journey. I imagined anything that would make me happy to have, or any place where I would love to be. I saw myself there and enjoyed every moment of it.

Exercises like this one helped me rest my mind and rejuvenate my whole body. I did them regularly and slowly started to develop peace and happiness.

Each time I traveled somewhere and put my feet on a new ground, I felt like a conquistador, without fear and without limits. I felt such deep pleasure and satisfaction. I loved to immerse into these new cultures and become someone new, melting into a new self. I loved to spend hours talking with the natives of each country, trying to understand them, trying to love them more. This was for me the only way of getting closer to them. It helped me learn to anticipate certain reactions, certain desires, certain fears. It helped me become better at business negotiations.

I had been in a large dynamic relational circle and was thriving in the middle of it. These people helped me open doors I could have never opened on my own. I was introduced to large conglomerates and large national companies that very few foreigners were able to approach. I had around me an autonomous business world that I was leading with the hand of a master. I felt on top of the world.

So please, to all of you out there with a brain, don't fall into the trap set by society. Stand out, believe and maintain standards that will create respect and growth. Fight for a certain quality level in anything you do, read or watch. Don't let your body and your soul float with the rivers of insanity and shame. Do the right thing for your childrfen and for the welfare of this world.

HAS THE TREND TOWARD REALITY TV IMPROVED THE QUALITY OF TELEVISION SHOWS? OF COURSE NOT. REALITY TV IS HAVING A DETRIMENTAL EFFECT ON THE QUALITY OF THE PROGRAMS OFFERED TO US. IT IS NOW CHALLENGING TO FIND PROGRAMS WITH SUBSTANCE. REALITY SHOWS HAVE GIVEN A JOB TO SECOND RATE PERFORMERS THAT ARE SPOILING OUR WORLD WITH THEIR POOR BEHAVIORS AND DISTURBING LANGUAGE.

I AM AFRAID TO THINK THAT THEY ARE SO POPULAR BECAUSE THEY ARE COMPLETELY DUMB, AND WE VIEWERS FEEL RATHER SUPERIOR. I GUESS IT IS SO CHALLENGING NOWADAYS TO FEEL SUPERIOR THAT WE FIND ANY EXCUSES TO FEEL GOOD. SO INSTEAD OF LOOKING UP, WE TAKE THE EASY ROAD, WE LOOK DOWN. WE ARE ALLOWING CHEAP ENTERTAINMENT TO FILL OUR SCREENS. WHAT IS SCARY IS THAT THEY MUST APPEAL TO THE MASSES AS THEIR POPULARITY IS GROWING. ARE YOU GOING TO LET THAT CONTINUE? WILL YOU KEEP WATCHING THOSE SHOWS OR WILL YOU START REACTING?

Always vote for principle, though you may vote alone, and you may cherish the sweetest reflection that your vote is never lost.
- John Quincy Adams

REALITY #13
POLITICS AND SOCIOECONOMICS

Politics is a subject very close to my heart. I grew up with a grandfather who was the mayor of one of the largest cities in France, Mulhouse. Emile Muller, his name, was the candidate of the Democratic Socialist Movement of France in the French presidential election in 1974. He was at first a member of the French Section of the Workers' International (SFIO), before leaving the party in 1970 to protest its alliance with the French Communist Party. He then founded the Party of Socialist Democracy (PDS), which participated in the Reforming Movement in 1972. In December 1973 he founded the Democratic Socialist Movement of France, or MDSF. The MDSF nominated him as its candidate in French presidential election. In 1981, he was succeeded by Joseph Klifa as mayor of Mulhouse. He had held the city since 1956. He also stepped down as deputy in 1981; he had represented the Haut-Rhin since 1958.

He died in 1988. I dearly miss him.

I remember spending many times listening to my grandfather speaking in front of huge crowds, moving them with his words and his beliefs, giving them the strength and the motivation to live good lives. He was fighting for people's rights. He wanted to create a balance between government control and entrepreneurship. He rejected extreme thinking as he had experienced extremism firsthand after being caught as a 4-year prisoner of the Germans led by Hitler during the second world war. I wish he was here today by my side to give me the guidance I need in these times of turmoil. In a way, I know he is here and I sometimes find myself with moments of wisdom I did not know I had. Papi, that must be you. I know that you would be outraged by what is happening today. We can't seem to get it right. Our politicians fight like children using decadent and dreadful words to destroy their opponents. They attack their families, their prides and put their hands on things that have nothing to do with politics. They act shamelessly trying to draw attention to them in whatever way they can. You see money laundering and millionaire politicians spending hundreds of millions in their campaigns, while 17% of people in the U.S. live below the poverty line, unable to feed their children, let alone keep a roof on top of their heads.

We are in a country where the political playing field is largely manipulated by the hands of massive corporations. Their intentions? To gain favor of the government and push for admittance of legislation they will benefit from. I call this corruption. This is exactly what my grandfather was fighting against. This is exactly what he refused to participate in. And this is exactly why he did not go very far in the presidential race. He was too ethical and never bent to bribery or surrounding corruptive behaviors.

Do you know that AT&T, the top contributor for the political spectrum from 1989-2010, spent $1.7 million total in the 1990 election cycle, yet twenty years later, spent $3 million in the 2010 election cycle, almost double their previous expenditures. The accumulated amount of cash raised by candidates for presidential campaigns, and the relation to the winner is simply another confirmation of the aforementioned surge of campaign financial support.

It seems like the financial backing of donors is what leads a candidate to victory. Is this the America you want to live in? A land where money is king and charismatic leaders can claim the crown? I don't know about you but I have a problem with that.

This is the vicious cycle of corruption in world politics. But is it just and is it right? No. Should it be stopped? Probably not stopped but definitely regulated. Without political funding, candidate names would never go very far. Yes, even Palin's house with the lake front view of Russia would not get it! Now, let's have a look at Sarah Palin as I think she is perfect representation of the trend or the "epidemic" that has taken place in our country. She was the Alaskan Governor and was called by McCain to become a Vice President mostly, let's face it, because she was an attractive dynamic woman. His strategy was bold and creative but not 100% efficient as he quickly lost credibility and the public's respect. Palin was fun to be around but very few trusted that she would be actually ready for the job.

On July 3, 2009, Palin announced she would not seek re-election as governor and that she was resigning effective July

26, 2009, eighteen months before the completion of her term. She cited ethics complaints that had been filed following her selection as running mate to John McCain as one of the reasons for her resignation, saying the resulting investigations had affected her ability to govern the state. Now we speculate that she will run for the Republican Party presidential nomination in 2012. That remains to be seen but considering all that has happened these last few years, absolutely not impossible.

Sarah, WOW. I am amazed by what you have been able to do. Fourty Seven years old and quite a path. Sarah is now the host of her own TV show called Sarah Palin's Alaska featuring her and her family experiencing adventure in Alaska and showing her everyday life. Well, you know what I think about reality shows, especially when they are meant to build your ego and your popularity mainly for political reasons. Let's be clear as this is the purpose of such show. Will it work? not impossible. Nothing would surprise me anymore. Time will tell.

We may or may not agree with what Sarah Palin is doing but I would like to point out a few facts and trends that I believe will help you rise to new levels as after all, that is the purpose of this book. Observe Sarah Palin very closely. Look at her attitude. Look at her energy. Look at how she holds herself and addresses crowds. Is she walking head low? Is she speaking softly? Is she shy and reserved or is she outgoing and loud? Is there a reason she is where she is? Why was she picked by Mr. McCain?

Sarah Palin reached the popularity and the "success" level that she currently knows for many reasons. She knows herself well. She has a determined walk. She dresses well and takes care of herself. She is attractive. She is proud and loud and unafraid of critics. She follows her path with strength and determination. She doesn't bend to pressure. She smiles all the time and most importantly she believes in herself. All of this shows. All of the afore-mentioned characteristics are what generates the energy that draws people to her. Whether we agree with her or not, you can't but notice the "noise" that she is making. We can even find ourselves watching her new reality show thinking it is quite charming and cute. Sarah knows how to reach crowds but most importantly she knows how to reach hearts and how to steer emotions. Do you think she would have known the same success had she been down and depressed with a grim on her face at all times? Absolutely not.

Sarah, I may not be in total agreement with your principals and political beliefs but I have to tell you that I admire your strength, your mental and your determination. I admire your going for it no matter what. No matter what people think or say, you do not bend to negative pressure. You have the courage to be who you are and to continue your journey.

This is what I'd like more women to do. We need to not be afraid. We need to believe in ourselves and build the new trends of tomorrow as tomorrow is our time. It is our time to shine, to grow, to build and to influence. It is our time to create variety, to paint new landscapes and to bring balance to a world that has been bending on one side for too long. We need all of you women to wake up and react and believe and dream as big as you possibly can.

I did some research on the number of women in national parliaments around the world as I believe countries that understand that a balance is needed in their parliament will grow healthier and stronger. Well I was quite surprised by what I found out. Here is the list of countries that have the lowest percentage of women in their Upper House or Senate next to their real GDP growth (2009 statistics):

		GDP per capita
• Yemen:	1.8%	$2,454
• Morocco:	2.2%	$4,587
• Kazakhstan:	4.3%	$11,679
• Congo:	4.6%	$4,136
• Russian Federation:	4.7%	$14,913
• Algeria:	5.1%	$6,885
• Romania:	5.8%	$11,869
• Poland:	8.0%	$18,050
• Nigeria:	8.3%	$2,274

Now here is the list of countries that have the highest percentage of women in their Upper House or Senate (2009 statistics):

• Bolivia:	47.0%	$4,451
• Burundi:	46.3%	$400
• Belgium:	42.5%	$35,534
• Senegal:	40.0%	$1,770
• South Africa	39.6%	$10,229

- Argentina: 35.2% $14,525
- Netherlands: 34.7% $39,877
- Canada: 34.4% $37,947
- Austria: 29.5% $38,567

And you have the in-between averages:

- Mexico: 19.5% $13,609
- Oman: 19.4% $25,635
- Italy: 18.3% $29,068
- Japan: 18.2% $32,554
- Lesotho: 18.2% $1,210
- United States of America: 15.3% $45,934
- Thailand: 16.0% $8,051

Now let me remind us all what GDP is. The gross domestic product (GDP) or gross domestic income (GDI) is the amount of goods and services produced in a year, in a country. It is the market value of all final goods and services made within the borders of a country in a year. It is often positively correlated with the standard of living. Gross domestic product comes under the heading of national accounts, which is a subject in macroeconomics.

Let's look at averages. The average GDP per capital of the countries that have the lowest percentage of women in their Upper House or Senate is $8,538. The average GDP per capital of the countries that have the highest percentage of women in their Upper House or Senate is $20,366. The average of the "in-between" is $24,187.

If you look at the charts on the next page, you notice clear trends. The "Low Group" that has the lowest percentage of women in their government also has the lowest GDPs per capita. Measuring GDP is complicated (which is why we leave it to the economists), but at its most basic, the calculation can be done in one of two ways: either by adding up what everyone earned in a year (income approach), or by adding up what everyone spent (expenditure method). Logically, both measures should arrive at roughly the same total.

What we clearly see is that countries with a low percentage of women in their government also have the lowest GDPs. Is that just a coincidence? Probably not as previous studies have proven the direct link between women's presence in a country's government and how well the country is doing economically.

Men and women are complementary to each other and bring different skill sets. If combined, the sum and total of those skill sets are stronger as more balanced and with a broader range of analysis, therefore bringing about better solutions.

We, women, have a social responsibility to be active in our communities and our governments. We need our voices to be stronger. We need to stop fearing expressing our views and we need to bring to the world the power within that can change what has never been changed before. Balance is key in anything. No government operates at its full potential without a variety of views and opinions expressed by both genders at all levels, equally.

My grandfather knew this. He was the proponent of balance and equality but was shut down for being too advanced in a society of human beings too comfortable in their old habits and too scared to dare to change.

As it takes guts to challenge the established. It takes courage to act and express views that may be regarded as unusual. However, no progress is made with the same old thinking. And no world-changing invention has been made by agreeable men and women.

Average %age of Women

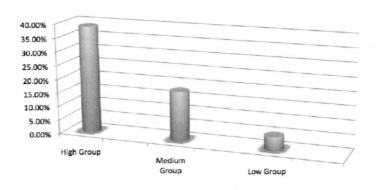

Average GDP per capita

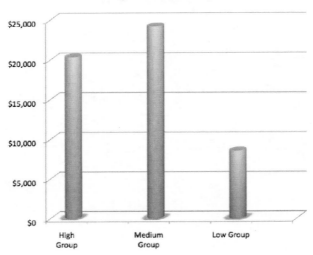

IN MANY COUNTRIES, WOMEN HAVE BEEN SOCIALIZED INTO BELIEVING THAT THE POLITICAL ARENA IS FOR MEN ONLY. THUS THEIR PARTICIPATION IN THE POLITICAL AND ELEC-TIVE OFFICE IS STILL AT VERY LOW LEVELS. DISCRIMINATION AGAINST GIRLS AND WOMEN IN THE DEVELOPING WORLD IS A DEVASTATING REALITY. IT RESULTS IN MILLIONS OF INDIVIDUAL TRAGEDIES, WHICH ADD UP TO LOST POTENTIAL FOR ENTIRE COUNTRIES. STUDIES SHOW THERE IS A DIRECT LINK BETWEEN A COUNTRY'S ATTITUDE TOWARD WOMEN AND ITS PROGRESS SOCIALLY AND ECONOMICALLY. THE STATUS OF WOMEN IS CENTRAL TO THE HEALTH OF A SOCIETY. IF ONE PART SUFFERS, SO DOES THE WHOLE.

Success is simply a matter of luck. Ask any failure.
- Earl Wilson

REALITY #14
BANKRUPTCY, FORECLOSURE, STARTING OVER

Bankruptcy is a concept I was never able to grab. I could never imagine going through something like that. I remember filling out the paperwork when I bought my first house asking if I had ever filed for bankruptcy. Whenever I was asked that question, I always said "no" thinking it was so obvious. Me filing for bankruptcy? That will never happen. I am educated and pretty smart. I will never find myself without work. I will always find a way to make money. I will always find ways to make the right choices to never have to go through bankruptcy. Not me!

Well was I wrong. Five years later, this is exactly what I had to do. I lived the American dream. I had come to this country with big dreams. I became and American citizen and wanted to experience all there was to experience. I had no fear. I built a business, invested in new technologies and went for it. I created interactive digital networks, I was featured in the local newspapers as an innovative entrepreneur, I was recognized among the five best start-ups in Nevada in 2008 and was honored by our Governor and I won national creative awards, I had it all! It took a little less than 8 months to make a big mess of all those accomplishments, mix them all in the cooking bowl, adding a little salt, a lot of pepper and a huge amount of spice to create the perfect mixture for bankruptcy.

I can now say that I have gone bankrupt. And I can now say it without any shame or hurt or regret. It is probably one of the best things that ever happened to me. I had no choice. I could have never paid back the loans that the company had and I wanted to have a chance to start over. That was my only option. But then reality hit.

June 2009.
In my house in Reno, Nevada.

It is dark outside. My mother just arrived from France. I had asked her to come as I needed help. Sitting on the front yard grass facing the mountains, it suddenly dawned on me that I no longer had my business, I no longer had a boyfriend and I was completely broke. I had lost everything. I had been in my house for 9 years and now I could not afford paying for it anymore as I was only getting unemployment money. During the past ten years, I had saved enough money to survive for a few years without working, I had put aside money for my daughter's college education, I had a 401K and an IRA that most people would have envied. Now, all (except for my IRA that I was able to keep) was gone. The bankruptcy took it all.

I was looking at the sky wondering what was next. I was asking God for guidance. I wanted to not lose faith in myself and in the world but somehow I knew I was heading towards difficult times. I knew that I was going to have to face the kind of storm I never faced before. The type that leaves you numb, forcing you to reposition into a universe that is unfamiliar and scary. My mother could not understand. Of course she couldn't. She never went through anything like this in her life.

I felt naked and wounded. Each wound grew and became intolerable. How many times did I find myself lying on the concrete, in the grass or on the rocks wanting my body to collapse deep into the soil. I wanted every cell of mine to melt into the sun until there was no more me. I think I felt ashamed. I saw myself as a failure. I had failed my daughter and I had failed my world. I wanted to cry but couldn't. My body was in a state of shock and nothing seemed to want to get out of it. I became a castle full of darkness with ghosts of hurt and sorrow haunting my vision, preventing me from getting up, from going forward, from reacting. I just wanted to die, to disappear and to never have to face such pain again. I felt nobody understood how hard it was for me. I was alone, so alone.

This state of desperation lasted a few weeks. I could not look for work, I had no more strength. My only goal was to build light in me again. I started to imagine building a candle that represented my life. Every day when I got up, I was envisioning life in that candle, lighting it up. Then I bought a real candle and every day, that's exactly what I did. I lit it up imagining it was my life that I was giving birth do. It was my life that I was looking at. Will I let the candle burn and die or will I replace it with bigger ones? Will I have to strength to light it up every day until I can jump and run again with joy. I was grieving. I was grieving for the life I had that I had lost. It was important for me to go through that grieving process and not rush it. I had to dive through the pain. I had to feel every fiber of my body recovering from that pain.

And then one day, I woke up and realized that yes, I had lost all of my physical belongings but I had not lost my soul. I had not lost my faith or my strengths. My body was healthy and my mind active. I was not paralyzed, I could express myself easily and clearly and I had to bounce back and start over. I had a wonderful healthy daughter that was working hard at school. A teenager without any problem. A girl dedicated to success and to happiness. As I watched her, I learnt . As I listened to her, I believed. As I kissed her good night, I knew that I had all the wealth in the world and that I had absolutely no right to complain and to be down again. It was now my duty to stand up, to walk towards new ventures believing in the rejuvenated, wiser world with a higher level of consciousness.

So I shook it up, got dressed like a pro and started looking for work. I answered ads and got hired in a local casino as marketing director within a month. Although that job did not work out as the casino world was not for me, it gave me faith. It showed me that I could get back on track. I found myself unemployed again for a few months. During that time, I consulted for a few companies. One of them hired me within a month of using their services. I am now still working for them and have been blessed. They have saved me. They have made me believe in myself again. I owe them my sanity.

In the meantime, I was losing my home and the foreclosure procedure was on its way. I hired an attorney to help me fight the banks that had not been willing to negotiate lower payments while I was out of work.

Of course, I have learnt a great deal along the way and here are the lessons I want to share with you:

1. Bankruptcy:

Before you decide to file for bankruptcy, hire a good attorney. I interviewed a few before I selected one. He became my angel and my guide and avoided me a lot of heartaches and a lot of expenses. I talked to him regularly. I was not alone.

Also, beware of the companies that say that they can reduce your debt by half if you pay them a certain amount of money every month. They are thief and liars. They don't do anything they say. It makes me sick that the TV stations play their ads as people believe in them. They use graphics that represent the government to lure people in a little faster. It is disgusting to me to see such practices happen and no one seem to prevent them from happening. Before I decided to file for bankruptcy, I fell into their trap but not for long as the little voice in me told me that something was wrong. They told me that if I paid them "just" $600 a month, they would reduce my debt by two. So then I started asking questions and they did not like it. I asked so what are you doing with the $600 I am paying you every month. Are you paying the creditors with it? Are you making payment plans with them? What is the deal? They always tried to elude the question by giving vague answers and ohhhh I did not like that. So I told them to cancel my contract with them and I investigated. I found out that they in fact place the money in an account and don't do anything with it for years. You read me well, I just said YEARS! Unbelievable. Then they contact the creditors and pay them partially. This is the biggest scheme on earth and it is still happening.

2. House foreclosure.

A record 2.22 million homes foreclosed in 2009. At least 3 million more homes entered foreclosure in 2010. 1 in 45 US homes was subject to at least one foreclosure filing, or 2.21% of all homes. Banks repossessed a record 918,000 homes in 2009, a 6.5 percent increase over 2008. There are now 5.5 million currently-delinquent mortgages. Home prices have fallen by 30% since October 2006. The doomsday prognostications say that 7 million properties are going to go back to the banks, all hitting the market at the same time, leading to a smoking crater. The $75 billion program offered banks rich incentives to renegotiate payment plans with their clients but ruled out reductions in mortgage principal, or outstanding loan balances. The banks refuse to take any loss on these vastly overvalued loans, despite the help they got from the government.

First time jobless benefit claims are still on the rise. The ratio of job seekers to open position is still about 11 to 1 and the pace of hiring is at lows not seen since data collection began ten years ago. The unemployment rate is of an average of 10 percent. Lay offs, job cuts and pay reductions are still very present and this touches all sectors from AOL to boat manufacturers. Amidst layoffs, wage cuts, rising prices, and rapidly deteriorating home values, consumers continue to cut back on spending.

The decrease in retail sales is likely to exacerbate the broader crisis. Consumer spending, a substantial proportion of which is retail sales, accounts for approximately two-thirds of US gross domestic product and is a major source of tax revenue for state and local governments.

Where are we heading? I somehow always felt that the "system" would protect me and allow me to find ways to recover from traumatic situations. I was wrong. The system, in this case, banks, have no interest in negotiating with you to find a solution that would allow you to get back on your feet and keep the home that you have been living in for years. They don't want to talk to you to enable you to keep a roof on your head and on your children's head so that you can at least maintain some sanity in all of this hardship. They forget that a home is the only safe haven that families still have in such times of crisis. By destroying this precious balance, they are damaging societal strength to overcome difficulties and improve our situations. Why? Because they are aiming directly at our prides and our hearts, destroying all that makes us who we are.

I have been in my house twelve years and had made all payments on time. Never missed one. And then things happened. My company went down and I found myself unemployed. I was not able to make payments anymore. I tried to contact the banks but they would not discuss any possible mortgage reduction. My bankruptcy filing preventing them from any action against me for a few months but when the bankruptcy proceedings were over and closed, the doors were open again for them to go after me. And they did.

So what did I do? I investigated what options I had as I was up for the fight. I refused to let go of my house so easily as I felt I had the right to do all that I could to try to keep it. After researching for days, I found out that I could do it on my own. A friend of mine recommended a good attorney specialized in foreclosure. So I called him and found out that he had kept 100% of his clients in their homes 2 years at least without having to make any payments while going through the foreclosure/mediation procedures with the banks.

He taught me that there are so many new laws protecting the homeowners that banks have a hard time getting all their paperwork in order to be able to fight the fight and kick the homeowners out of their homes. One mediation can follow the next until banks finally come up with all that is needed to go to the next step. And this can take months. What makes me sick to my stomach is that they are getting those homes back and then having short sales on them. They end up losing money anyway. This is totally absurd. Any decent society would help each other in a good samaritan way. Banks would be negotiating principal reductions and allow home owners to get back on their feet. But on the contrary, they ignore the pain and kick straight into the wound, without any remorse or regret.

The government helped them but they refuse to help

back. They are not returning the service. The system is rotten and anything rotten ends up with a terrible smell that can take years to go away. Unless banks start getting back some common sense, we are going to see a society in decline because its people will have lost faith and strength to continue the "good" fight instead of being caught in a fight they know they will lose at one point in time.

I am still in my home just starting the mediation procedure and hope to be in here for another year at least before I am kicked out and forced to go rent somewhere else. Or it may also turn out that the bank will offer me to rent my own home.

No matter what, I am outraged by such nonsense and have no conscience problem doing all that I can to make it difficult for them to accomplish their goals. It is unfair. It is unethical. It goes again a healthy societal conscience.

IF YOU ARE IN THE SAME SITUATION, FIGHT THE FIGHT. DO NOT GIVE UP TO THEIR FEAR TACTICS. BANKS WILL SCARE YOU BY POSTING NOTICES ON YOUR HOME AND SENDING YOU DOZEN OF THREATENING LETTERS. HIRE A GOOD ATTORNEY AND MOST IMPORTANTLY REMEMBER THAT UNETHICAL TACTICS ARE BEING USED, AND JUST LIKE THE SUN LEAVES SPACE FOR THE MOON AT NIGHT, DARKNESS WILL IN TURN REACH THEM AS WELL IN DUE TIME, AS WHAT GOES AROUND COMES AROUND. ALWAYS.

You must not lose faith in humanity. Humanity is an ocean; if a few drops of the ocean are dirty, the ocean does not become dirty.
                                   - Mohandas Gandhi

REALITY #15
USE YOUR STAR POWERS

To understand the very large, we must understand the very small.

To understand and appreciate who you truly are, you must realize that you are complex and extraordinary in each and every one of your cells. Your body is made of seven octillion atoms. That is seven followed by 27 zeros: 7000000000000000000000000000.

There is 99.9999999999% of empty space in an atom. This means that we humans are mostly made of empty space and so is the universe. The big (the universe) is what made the small (you) and they are both similar and one. They both have the same properties, the same capabilities, the same strength.

Now you must wonder what gives us any substance if we are mostly emptiness. It is the electromagnetic force of the atom that creates everything. We never really touch anything. All is energy. We are energy. Have you read ***The***

Secret or watched the video? That is the main message. Our energy (whether positive or negative) is what creates our lives. Our energy is what attracts the good or the bad.

Scientists have learnt a lot about atoms and have now reached the level of nanotechnology that is expected to deliver a lot of new things to our everyday lives. As an example, nano-diamonds will soon replace syringes to administer medicine in our body. What is amazing is that they could potentially soon cure cancer as nano-diamonds can find the sick cells in the body and kill them, leaving all healthy cells intact. Is that fascinating or what? The universe was created 36.7 billion years ago. The world was initiated by an explosion of a star. Our bodies are composed of star stuff and every atom was at some point part of a star. This means that you and I at some point were a star. Stars created us. We are stars!

Oxygen in water is the remnant of star explosions. This means that the water we drink is made of bits of dinosaurs and bits of people who lived before us. Each time we breathe in, we breathe in molecules that a lot of other humans breathed in before we were even born: Socrates, Galileo, Picasso, Einstein, Eisenhower. Imagine how much knowledge and talent we can potentially breathe in without knowing it! All what I am telling you is pure science, not imagination. All of this is the result of research done in nano- and nuclear science.

We are in a continual process of creation. The universe

is dominated by extreme sizes. The structure of the very large is the same as the structure of the very small. We can piece together answers on who we truly are when we understand that principle. We, as small as we can be in comparison to the universe, have the same power. You, as small as you think you may be, have the power to move mountains. You can change anything you want if you decide to. Again, this is science not a hypothesis I just made to make you feel good.

The moon was born from a gigantic collision between the earth and a planet as big as Mars. That collision created millions of rocks, big and small that were thrown into the atmosphere and one of them slowly built itself into what we now know as the moon.

Why am I speaking about science? Because I believe it is important for you and I to remember to look at our life and its events from a broader perspective to understand why things are happening the way they are. Science also teaches us that collisions and impacts are the universal ways of putting everything back together. After all, the impacts of the universe is the reason why we are here today. Dinosaurs were dominant and killing everything around them when an asteroid hit and destroyed the earth. Human life would not have been possible then. But the impact allowed new life to take place. Animals and humans were then able to survive longer than just a few days as they would have just been dinosaur food.

We live in times of turbulence and clash at many levels where everything is questioned. I believe (and this is now my view of things, not proven science) that the collision we are experiencing nowadays is one created by an imbalance that grew over the years from various abuses of systems, from neglects of principles and from disregard of our fundamental support, the earth. Considering that all of this is pure energy, we generated over the years electromagnetic forces that could not withstand each other for very long. We created negative energies that could not balance out with the positive ones. It resulted in a universal/atomic explosion embodied by a deep economic and financial crisis. The asteroid that hit us was made of corruption, lies, abuse, ignorance and disregard of the true essentials that kept us safe.

Of course, this is the not the end of the world. What did science say before? That collisions and impacts are the universal ways of putting everything back together. So here is something else I believe in. I believe that we are now living the aftermath of one of the biggest collisions we have known in our lifetime. We are still a little light-headed and scared, looking for the balance we have lost. We are still wondering how to walk straight again and how to not want to hide behind our fears. This is a process that takes time but it will go faster if you understand why you are going through it. It will become easier if you know that this was inevitable and that it was all energy generated by all that is.

You can now use your energy to change whatever you want and become the star that in essence you already are. Become aware of it. Realize your powers and your strengths and stop being scared of failures and defeats. The universe is showing us that they are necessary to our balance and our growth. What you see as your own failures is in fact your chance to become a better you and to have a better life.

Dream it, see it, feel it, every single day going forward and your stardom will slowly build itself around its extraordinary nucleus: YOU.

COLLISIONS AND IMPACTS ARE THE UNIVERSAL WAYS OF PUTTING EVERYTHING BACK TOGETHER. THE IMPACTS OF THE UNIVERSE ARE THE REASON WHY WE ARE HERE TODAY. WE HUMANS ARE MOSTLY EMPTY SPACE. EMPTY SPACE IS LIGHT AND EASY TO MOVE. LET'S NOT SLOW DOWN BY IMAGINATIVE WALLS. LET'S FLOAT IN THE AIR AND FLY LIGHT TOWARDS OUR DREAMS. LET'S BE THE STARS THAT WE KNOW WE ARE AND ACCOMPLISH GREAT AND GRAND THINGS, NOW.

"In my life I had come to realize that when things were going very well indeed it was just the time to anticipate trouble. And, conversely, I learned from pleasant experience that at the most despairing crisis, when all looked sour beyond words, some delightful "break" was apt to lurk just around the corner."
- Amelia Earhart

4.
WORLD FACTS FOR A REAL SHOT OF ST. JOHN'S WORT MORALE BOOSTER

You think you have it bad? You feel powerless and desperate with no way out? Here are facts that made me shift my thinking and realize that after all, it could be much, much worse.

Women in many parts of the world have no power, no freedom, living daily discrimination and forced to slavery. While women in the United States and Europe often measure sex discrimination by pay scales and seats in corporate board rooms, women in the Third World gauge discrimination by mortality rates and poverty levels.

From South America to South Asia, women are often subjected to a lifetime of discrimination with little to no hope of relief. As little girls, they aren't fed as well as boys and are denied education and hospitalization in case they get ill. As teenagers, most of them are forced into marriage, sometimes bought and sold for prostitution and slave labor. As wives and mothers, they are treated little better than farm-hands. Should they outlive their husbands, they are denied inheritance, banished from their homes and forced to live as beggars on the streets.

In the developing world, there is a social and cultural attitude where women are viewed as inferior. A woman's biggest challenge is simply surviving. In South Asia and China, the dangers begin at birth, with the threat of infanticide. Sociologists and government officials began documenting sporadic examples of female infanticide in India about ten years ago. The practice of killing newborn girls is largely a rural phenomenon in India. Surveys showed that more than half of the women had killed baby daughters.

In India, a young woman is regarded as a temporary member of her natural family and a drain on its wealth. Her parents are considered caretakers whose main responsibility is to deliver a chaste daughter, along with a sizable dowry, to her husband's family. In India, about one-fourth of the 12 million girls born each year die by age 15.

Surviving childbirth is itself an achievement in South Asia for both mother and baby. One of every eighteen women dies of a pregnancy-related cause, and more than one of every ten babies dies during delivery. For female children, the survival odds are even worse. Almost one in every five girls born in Nepal and Bangladesh dies before the age 5. Women are often hospitalized only when they have reached a critical stage of illness, which is one reason so many mothers die in childbirth. Female children often are not hospitalized at all.

Statistics from Pakistan demonstrate the low priority given to female education: Only one-third of the country's schools ~ which are sexually segregated ~ are for women, and one-third of those have no building. Almost 90 percent of the women over age twenty five are illiterate.

Across South Asia, arranged marriages are the norm and can sometimes be the most demeaning rite of passage a woman endures. Two types are common: bride wealth, in which the bride's family essentially gives her to the highest bidder, and dowry, in which the bride's family pays huge amounts to the husband's family. This practice by the way is also the case in many African countries. In some countries, dowries are extravagant, costing years' worth of wages, and often throwing a woman's family into debt. The dowry practice makes the prospect of having a girl even more distasteful to poor families. It also puts young women in danger:

In India, many men resort to killing their wives ~ often by setting them afire ~ if they are unhappy with the dowry. UNICEF estimates that around 5,000 Indian women are killed in dowry-related incidents each year.

Sex-selective abortions are even more common than infanticides in India. They are growing ever more frequent as technology makes it simple and cheap to determine a fetus' gender. In Jaipur, a Western Indian city of 2 million people, 3,500 sex-determined abortions are carried out every year. The gender ratio across India has dropped to an unnatural low of 927 females to 1,000 males due to infanticide and sex-based abortions.

In Kenya and Tanzania, laws prohibit women from owning houses. Women in every society are vulnerable to abuse. But the threat is more severe for girls and women who live in societies where women's rights mean practically nothing. Mothers who lack their own rights have little protection to offer their daughters, much less themselves, from male relatives and other authority figures. The frequency of rape and violent attacks against women in the developing world is alarming. Forty-five percent of Ethiopian women say that they have been assaulted in their lifetimes. In 1998, 48 percent of Palestinian women admitted to being abused by an intimate partner within the past year.

In Pakistan, a daughter legally is entitled to half the inheritance that a son gets when their parents die. In some criminal cases, testimony by women is legally given half the weight of a man's testimony, and compensation for the wrongful death of a woman is half that for the wrongful death of a man.

In North Korea, women can be forced into marriage or the sex industry. The methods by which traffickers recruit women are deception, coercion and abduction. Although many women try to escape from their exploitative situation, others do not. Testimonies from trafficked women indicate that many remain because they feel helpless and powerless to change their situation.

In the case of forced marriages, some women choose to

stay because of the birth of a child and/or they have developed an emotional attachment to their husband. Several women trafficked into forced marriage and the sex industry have expressed the view that despite everything, their current situation is better than risking repatriation or starvation. Many North Korean women allow a third party to sell them as brides to Chinese men or agree to an arranged marriage. Marriages involving undocumented North Korean women, however, are not legally binding and if the women are caught by the Chinese authorities, they - like any other irregular North Korean migrant - face deportation.

In some cultures, the physical and psychological trauma of rape is compounded by an additional stigma. In cultures that maintain strict sexual codes for women, if a woman steps out of bounds—by choosing her own husband, flirting in public, or seeking divorce from an abusive partner—she has brought dishonor to her family and must be disciplined. Often, discipline means execution. Families commit "honor killings" to salvage their reputation tainted by disobedient women.

According to UNICEF, nine million more girls than boys miss out on school every year. While their brothers continue to go to classes or pursue their hobbies and play, they join the women to do the bulk of the housework. Housework in developing countries consists of continuous, difficult physical labor. A girl is likely to work from before daybreak until the light drains away. She walks barefoot long distances several times a day carrying heavy buckets of water, most likely polluted, just to keep her family alive. She cleans, grinds corn, gathers fuel, tends to the fields, bathes her younger siblings, and prepares meals until she sits down after all the men in the family have eaten. Most families can't afford modern appliances, so her tasks must be done by hand—crushing corn into meal with heavy rocks, scrubbing laundry against rough stones. There is no time left in the day to learn to read and write or to play with friends. She collapses exhausted each night, ready to wake up the next morning to start another long workday.

Most of this labor is performed without recognition or reward. UN statistics show that although women produce half the world's food, they own only 1 percent of its farmland. In most African and Asian countries, women's work isn't even considered real labor. Should a woman take a job, she is expected to keep up all her responsibilities at home in addition to her new ones, with no extra help.

More than 130 million women and girls alive today have been subjected to female genital mutilation/cutting (FGM/C), which can have grave health consequences, including the failure to heal, increased susceptibility to HIV infection, childbirth complications, inflammatory diseases and urinary incontinence.

I will stop here. You got the picture. Are you still feeling down or did a little learning about what a lot of women in this world are going through help? Well I certainly hope it did as it helped me create a definite perspective about my situations. Suddenly, my pains and my fears diminished and I knew my world was open. I knew that I was free to change and to move.

I knew I had the liberty to study, express myself and challenge.

I now hope that whenever you feel down, desperate or depressed, you remember those world facts about what women have to endure in their daily lives in certain parts of our world and you will know that after all, it could be much, much worse.

YOU DON'T KNOW WHAT TOMORROW BRINGS
SO BE THE NOW AND ENJOY YOUR SWINGS
FOR NOW IS TIME FOR YOUR SMILE TO SHINE
AND FOR YOUR SOUL TO RISE IN INCLINE
SURROUND YOUR TEMPLE WITH WHOLESOME HEARTS
AND SOON YOU'LL SEE FULL POSITIVE CHARTS
LOVE YOURSELF, ALL ANIMALS AND NATURE
FOR THEY ARE BEAUTY, SERENITY AND LAUGHTER
THEY WILL SHOW YOU PEACE, JOY AND HUMOR
AND PROVE THAT IN THE END IT'S ALL ABOUT HONOR
HONOR THE WORLD, THE UNIVERSE AND ALL THAT IS
AS WE ARE ONE SO BE APPEASED
LET YOUR FEARS MELT IN THE RAYS OF THE SUN
AND SOON YOU'LL SEE HOW MUCH LIFE IS FUN
DON'T LET YOUR PAST DRAW YOUR NEW PATHS
JUST REMEMBER AND SURRENDER TO THE AFTERMATH
SHINE MY FRIENDS AND SMILE WITH PRIDE
FOR YOU ARE THE TREASURE OF THIS INCREDIBLE RIDE

EPILOGUE

If you want to face a beautiful sunset, you have to face West. No matter how talented you are, if you face East, you will never see it.

Don't let your circumstances dictate your life and consume you. They are not you. They are just "stuff" that happened to you and they will pass like the storm flies through the meadows. You on the contrary won't. You are here to stay and to be as fully as you possibly can.

Your beliefs have taken you to where you are today. Start building something instead of trying to just save yourself. Determine your dreams and stay committed to them. How do you want to live? Make an honest answer.

Live with passion, with the burning desire for something. Passion is thinking right. When you think right, you attract the right people to you and when I say the right people, I mean the people you need the most and that will contribute to your personal and spiritual growth.

Work on your belief. Learn to be resistant and not to worry. Ask yourself: "what's the worst that could happen to me?" Look at yourself from afar, with perspective and wisdom and always remember that there is much worse happening in the world. Do not hold on to an identity that does not make you happy. The sum total of your life is today. Can you be the same woman forever or do you want to experience greatest level of joy and happiness?

Dream big, thing high of yourself, love yourself first, and love others. Always walk head high. Treat others well. Treat animals and nature well. Express respect to all that is around you and you will get back in trillions. Trust me. Do it.

I dream to be able to help you become master of you. I want you to let yourself dream so that you can win. I want you to give birth to true happiness and as you know, the birth process is painful but so rewarding!

When you are in pain going through labor, you can't think enough of the outcome of your pain and it hurts. It hurts so much you want to scream and you don't know how you are going to go through that pain and survive it.

In the same fashion, giving birth to the new you is equally painful. You are and will be often in such pain that you won't be able to see the light at the end of the tunnel. However, if you fight long enough and stay focused (you want the baby out after all, don't you?) then you keep pushing and believing as you know the result (the baby) is going to feel amazing, incredible. When the head is out, your belief strengthens as you start seeing the light at the end of the tunnel, don't you? So you push and you push and you force yourself to do it and to move forward. I can't imagine you saying at that point of the birth process that you want to remain at that stage because you are scared to continue and that you have no more strength. That would not be too comfortable, would it? Even worse, you would probably kill not only yourself but your baby. So you make an extra effort and you go for it and then comes the baby and you forget about everything that you just went through because the result feels so wonderful. It is another world, a new life.

Remember the parallel I have just made between you giving birth to a child and your life, and as you go through pain and cry and hurt and want to give up. Remember though that if you give up, you may die. So think of the outcome. Think about the light at the end of the tunnel. Think that in order to reach that light, you will have to go through a certain level of darkness and that the road may be bumpy. But don't give up.

Continue and believe that you can.

Soon, when you reach the light, you will look back and know it was all necessary. It was all worth it. You will then understand that you had to go through that journey to reach the point where you are at.

As for me, things have started to turn around. I feel strong and more determined than ever. Positive energies have started to invade my body and soul and I am ready to climb the highest mountains, to experience the biggest joys and to live life as fully as I have ever imagined.

After working as an employee for a couple of companies that were wonderful enough to hire me, I realized that my calling was to own my own business. Now that I already had gained one experiene doing it a few years ago, I felt much more comfortable this time around. I developed a niche, made contacts and there I was on the road to entrepreneurship, again. When it's truly in you, it's nowhere else.

My second husband, Larry, has grown to be a wonderful father to Adelle. He has found balance in his life and has been able to grow to become her coach and her male role model. He has enabled her to develop respect for men that will be so essential for her future well-being as a wife and mother. His parents have never stopped being outstanding grand-parents. They have provided Adelle with the warmth of a true family, always here for her.

Adelle's birth father still has no clue about real life values. Although he claimed to be disciplined follower of his faith, he forgot that true faith is much more than following a strict diet or going to the synagogue daily. He has forgotten that he had a role to play as a father and that, as such, had certain duties and obligations, both moral and financial. My principles led me to sue him for child custody after fifteen years of not asking for a dime. I hope that Adelle gets what she deserves and I also hope that, some day, he wakes up to realize how much he has missed. Regrets will certainly weigh heavily on his death bed. But then, it will be too late.

Blessings to you. May you create wonders.

May you be remembered as an incredible individual that took chances and gave it all to this incredible adventure called life.

And remember, when one tale ends, another begins.

Love always.

Catherine

HERE ARE SOME OF MY PAINTINGS OF WHAT WE WOMEN MUST STRIVE TO REPRESENT

Fortunella

The Modern Joconde.
Her body is half tree, half bird.
She represents stability, peace and strength.
She sees the world with one eye
that never deviates for her goals and dreams.

Antiopa

The Accomplished Contessa in Love with a Rooster.

She endured bumpy rides but lives now
in a castle of love.
Embracing her uniqueness, she is fully
and demands respect. If she does not get it,
she walks away with no shame, no anger,
keeping her determination for happiness.

Metameria

Butterflies flying from the Heart to the Moon

She is in love with someone she can't have.
She knows it is not right and fights to forget and
to redirect herself to righteous paths.
Her will pushes the butterflies to leave her
heart and disappear in the darkness of the
nights towards the shining moon.

Skeria

The Bird's Enabler Holding the Ocean in her Hands

She is in control of her world. She helps animals thrive
and shares unlimited love with the universe.
She smiles always and believes in the impossible.
Nature is her guide. She finds in it balance,
serenity and extreme joy.

Fetherelle

The Ocean Spy Learning from the Wise Goose

She knows the secret of the universe. She has traveled the world and secretly guides women in search of their path. The Goose is her best friend. She shares with her wisdom and messages from the deep, deep world taking us to higher levels of happiness.

For more on my art, please visit:
http://www.catherineoaks.com/art.html

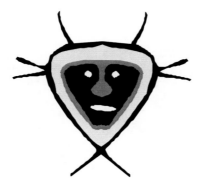